Performance Evaluation of SLPEs in Karnataka

Published by
ACADEMIC FOUNDATION
in association with

Institute of Public Enterprise

Performance Evaluation of SLPEs in Karnataka

Editors

R.K. Mishra

S.S. Subrahmanyam

ACADEMIC FOUNDATION

NEW DELHI

www.academicfoundation.com

First published in 2014
by

ACADEMIC FOUNDATION
4772-73 / 23 Bharat Ram Road, (23 Ansari Road),
Darya Ganj, New Delhi - 110 002 (India).
Phones : 23245001 / 02 / 03 / 04.
Fax : +91-11-23245005.
E-mail : books@academicfoundation.com
www.academicfoundation.com

in association with

Institute of Public Enterprise, Hyderabad

Disclaimer:
The findings/views/opinions expressed in this book are solely those of the authors and do not necessarily reflect the views of the publisher.

Cataloging in Publication Data--DK
Courtesy: D.K. Agencies (P) Ltd. <docinfo@dkagencies.com>

Performance evaluation of SLPEs in Karnataka / editors, R.K. Mishra, S.S. Subrahmanyam.
p. cm.
Contributed articles.
ISBN 9789332701410

1. Government business enterprises--India--Karnataka--Evaluation. 2. Karnataka Neeravari Nigam Limited.--Evaluation. I. Mishra, R. K., 1948- II. Subrahmanyam, S. S. III. Title: Performance evaluation of state level public enterprises in Karnataka.

DDC 338.62095487 23

Typeset by Italics India, New Delhi.

Printed and bound by The Book Mint, New Delhi.
www.thebookmint.in

Contents

List of Tables and Figures

Tables

Figures

About the Editors/ Contributors

Editors:

Ram Kumar Mishra, Director, Institute of Public Enterprise (IPE), Hyderabad, is a graduate from the International Management Programme, SDA Bocconi, Milan, Italy, and a fellow of the British Council and the Commonwealth Secretariat. He has been working on key assignments with Indian government including the Performance Management Division, Cabinet Secretariat, Ministries of HRD, Power, Trade and Commerce, Heavy Industry & Public Enterprises, and Finance (Department of Disinvestment). He has also been a researcher for Planning Commission, Finance Commission, Prime Minister's Economic Advisory Council, State Bureaus of Public Enterprises, financial institutions and banks. He has supervised more than 70 doctoral researchers and his current areas of interest include: performance management, corporate finance, corporate governance, restructuring, economic reforms, social sector management and good governance.

S.S. Subrahmanyam has over 37 years of industrial, financial, venture capital and consulting experience, out of which last 22 years had been in senior and middle management positions. He was associated with a large public finance institution as an executive dealing with business promotion, entrepreneurial selection, project appraisals, venture capital funding, equity balancing, budgeting, strategic planning, project management, taxation policies and procedures, mergers & acquisitions—to mention a few, apart from other routine senior management functions such as people management, performance appraisals, build and motivate teams, etc. He has also worked at a leading public sector machine tool company dealing with production, planning, operations management, methods engineering, systems analysis, etc. During his tenure of around 17 years at Andhra Pradesh Industrial Development Corporation (APIDC, a State Government owned financial institution), he had been closely associated with innumerable and varied clientele in different traditional sectors—industry and trade, finance, health care, infrastructural sectors—power, telecommunications, energy—and high technology sectors—software, biotechnology. Presently, he is working for IPE as a Senior Consultant providing expertise for design and implementation & training.

Contributors:

J. Kiranmai, Assistant Professor, Institute of Public Enterprise, Hyderabad.

A. Pawan Kumar, Assistant Professor, Institute of Public Enterprise, Hyderabad.

Lakshmi Kumari, Assistant Professor, Institute of Public Enterprise, Hyderabad.

S.K. Mathur, Senior Faculty, Institute of Public Enterprise, Hyderabad.

V. Srikanth, Assistant Professor, Institute of Public Enterprise, Hyderabad.

Preface

SLPEs constitute an important component of the public enterprise system in India. SLPEs are known as sub-national public enterprises. To study their functioning, it is in order to take up a case study as to how they operate in a particular state. It is in this context that we have taken up Karnataka SLPEs for the case study. The present volume is a collection of eight case studies on the performance evaluation of SLPEs in Karnataka. The enterprises selected for the case studies are: Hutti Gold Mines Ltd, Karnataka Power Transmission Corporation Ltd, Karnataka State Police Housing Corporation, Bangalore Metropolitan Corporation Ltd, Hubli Electricity Company Ltd, Karnataka Neeravari Nigam Ltd, Horticultural Producers Cooperative Marketing and Processing Society, and Karnataka State Agricultural Marketing Board.

The volume highlights the key challenges of public sector reforms faced by the Government of Karnataka and its approach to tackle these challenges. The book will be useful to policy makers, public enterprise managers and researchers engaged in the SLPEs reforms to take a fresh look at the strategies and approaches to attend to the problems being faced by the SLPEs. Although Maharashtra had initiated the SLPEs reforms in 1990s, the Government of Karnataka has followed suit by taking bold measures. The turnaround in the profitability of some of the SLPEs in Karnataka adequately supports this contention.

Study Methodology

Background of the Report

The Department of Public Enterprises (DPE), Government of Karnataka (GoK), is aimed at evaluating the performance of both physical and financial aspects of the state level public enterprises (SLPEs) and also to examine the aspects for restructuring of evaluated SLPEs in order to strengthen the public sector units. The study and evaluation of SLPEs also help the public enterprises to perform better in the future. As per the Medium Term Fiscal Plan of GoK for 2001-02 to 2004-05, one of the key measures identified for phasing out revenue deficit and reducing of fiscal deficit, was reduction of budgetary support to the public enterprises and other measures such as curtailing revenue expenditure so as to improve its physical parameters, restructuring of the organisation to generate more profits, etc. This was proposed to be achieved by disinvesting and restructuring public enterprises. The plan acknowledges that while in some cases it may be necessary to introduce voluntary retirement scheme (VRS) to reduce over-employment, government may have to close down or privatise some of the enterprise. The policy was framed to sustain the economic growth through private partnerships. Thus, the key intent behind public sector enterprises (PSEs) reforms in Karnataka is reduction of financial burden on the state exchequer on account of SLPEs.

With a view to minimising the procedural delays involved in taking an objective view and resolving the issues associated with disinvestments of SLPEs, the GoK had set up a separate department *viz.,* Department of Disinvestments and State Public Sector Enterprises Reforms (DDPER) in 2002. This was subsequently renamed as Department of Public Enterprises (DPE) in 2006. DPE is the apex body taking all the decisions regarding SLPES. The key functions and tasks of DPE are listed below:

- Assist the government in carrying out the evaluation of performance of SLPEs and recommend appropriate measures for restructuring of unviable or non-performing SLPEs.
- Evolving criteria for evaluation of the SLPEs considering the need and relevance of the SLPEs, sustainable profitability of the SLPEs and financial liability of the state.
- Develop action plan for restructuring of the SLPEs.
- Develop action plan for rationalisation of employment in the SLPEs, ensuring that the interests of the labour are adequately safeguarded.

Terms of Reference

The terms of reference for the study are:

- To study in depth and suggest useful action point for improving the efficiency of the organisation/restructure the organisation, if necessary.
- The study should cover whether the PSE is enable to compete with similar other SLPEs or similar private sector undertakings (PSUs).
- To determine whether the company is contributing towards corporate social responsibility (CSR) and GDP of Karnataka.
- To determine whether the PSE has any potential to create employment to the people for Karnataka.
- To establish that the SLPEs are utilising their resources optimally.
- To determine the overall performance and the working atmosphere of the organisation and establish whether the PSE is people friendly and eco-friendly.
- To determine whether the 10 per cent disinvestment of the organisation is possible.

Caveats

The report may be read in consideration of the following caveats:

- Our understanding of the work of SLPEs based on discussions. The scope of study is not a thorough audit of the organisation and hence, the data submitted after preliminary validation have been considered for analysis.
- Audited accounts have been used till 2006-07 and verified accounts of 2007-08 have been used.
- Institute of Public Enterprises (IPE) has made recommendations for taking into account the various alternatives that lead to budgetary provision of state government. The recommendations include various major steps including possible capital restructuring of the enterprise by marginal investment.
- The scope of work includes the following:
    - o Discussion with the managing director, company secretary and other heads of department.
    - o Discussion with the employees of organisation.
- The outputs and recommendations of the study will not, in any manner, be deemed to constitute a legal or a tax opinion, nor will they be substituted for either of them.
- The scope of the study did not include detailed study of other organisations for possible merger/amalgamations and synergies thereof.
- The market outlook in this report is based on the conditions prevailing at the time of the study. The report is purely recommendatory in nature.

Methodology Adopted for the Study

- Discussion were held with the managing director, company secretary and other heads of department of SLPEs.
- Case study based methodology has been adopted.

- Detailed discussion were held with the other divisions head of SLPEs, with the objectives of evaluating the overall operational performance, success in achievement of stated objectives within time frame, management structure, key process, etc.
- Working atmosphere of the organisation was evaluated to study, whether the organisation exists in a people friendly and an eco-friendly atmosphere.
- Ascertaining that the organisation utilises its resources optimally.
- Evaluating that the company is contributing towards corporate social responsibility and GDP of Karnataka, and also has potential to create employment for the people of Karnataka.

1 State Level Public Enterprises in Karnataka

An Overview

R.K. Mishra

Introduction

Karnataka is one of the high economic growth states in India with gross state domestic product (GSDP) of US$ 58.23 billion in 2008-09, at current prices. On the sectoral contribution front, the tertiary sector contributed US$ 31.6 billion (55%), followed by the secondary sector at US$ 17 billion (29%) and the primary sector contributed US$ 9.5 billion (16%) to the GSDP in 2008-09. With the establishment of largest public sector, industries like Hindustan Aeronautics Limited, National Aerospace Laboratories, Bharat Heavy Electricals Limited, Indian Telephone Industries, Bharat Earth Movers Limited, Bharat Electronics Limited, Hindustan Machine Tools, etc., the state has evolved as the manufacturing hub of India.

The state has had a strong tradition of state sector-led industrialisation. Moving on to the state level public sector enterprises (SLPEs) in Karnataka, the princely state of Mysore, which was quite rich in natural resources, had started its industrial activities before India's independence (Mendon, 1964).[1] The noteworthy initiatives of Sir M. Visveshvarayya, like Mysore Iron Works (later the Mysore Iron and Steel Works), the Mysore Sugar Factory, the Mysore Soap Factory, the Mysore Paper Mills and the Mysore Silk Weaving Factory, etc., created employment and generated other economic spin-offs. Bangalore owes much of its development to the establishment of several state public sector enterprises (PSEs) in the 1950s. After independence, the state government of Karnataka successively expanded the horizons of SLPEs in the state.

1. Mendon, D.K. (1964). *Industrial Mysore*. Bombay: Tainudi Publications.

The present paper analyses the current status of SLPEs in Karnataka, their performance and highlights various recent government policy measures for the development of these enterprises in the state.

The Growth Story

On an analysis of the growth of the SLPEs in Karnataka as it can be observed from Figure 1.1 that 10 (23% of total enterprises) PSEs were set up during the 5th Five Year Plan. The period during 1985-2007 can be termed as a remarkable period for the public sector in Karnataka, because about 33 enterprises were established during this period. The total number of enterprises went up to 65 by the end of 2008. The current status of enterprises in the state does not include the enterprises which have been wound up or merged with others. It has also been observed that mostly the enterprises were set up in the manufacturing and welfare sectors.

Figure 1.1

Plan-wise Growth of SLPEs in Karnataka

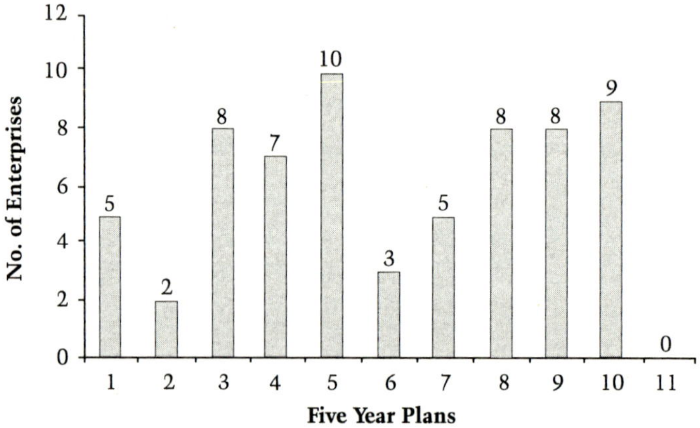

Source: Comptroller & Auditor General (CAG) (Commercial), Government of India (GoI) and author's calculations.

Overview of SLPEs

Karnataka occupies third place among the working SLPEs in India. Over the years, the enterprises have developed gradually. There were 65 working SLPEs in Karnataka as on 31 March, 2008. Nearly 67 per cent of the enterprises were making profits and 20 per cent were incurring losses. The total investment was ₹ 4,7813.29 crore, consisting of paid-up capital and long term loans. The capital employed increased by 7.6 per cent in 2007-08. The total number of employees were 1.69 lakh, which increased by 5.8 per cent in 2007-08. The turnover increased by 10 per cent from ₹ 25,284.68 crore in 2006-07 to ₹ 28,218.05 crore in 2007-08. The SLPEs in Karnataka made a profit of ₹ 996.02 crore in 2007-08. The details are given in Table 1.1.

Table 1.1

Overview of SLPEs in Karnataka

(₹ in lakh)

Particulars	*2007-08*	*2006-07*	*2005-06*
Investment			
Paid-up capital			
State Government	2330987	2069938	1847734
Central Government	29780.36	15980.36	12980.36
Others	30686.47	32185.21	26634.45
Total	2391466	2118104	1887349
Long Term Loan			
Government	746453.8	702706.4	694972.9
Others	1643409	1606328	1569142
Total	2389863	2309035	2264114
Total Investment	4781329	4427138	4151463
Capital employed	5159088	4766086	4873473
Turnover	2821805	2528468	2104271
Net Profit/Loss	99602.06	93472.51	60570.79
Accumulated profit/loss	214831.4	182459.5	210566.3
No. of Employees	168811	159104	156480
Total Return on Capital employed	250963	235283.5	179999.2
Percentage of total return on capital employed	787.96	627.6	662.19
Subsidies/Grants			
Central Government	26651.61	7921.23	1300.64
State Government	230379.5	623621.6	307951.9
Total	257031.1	631542.8	309252.5

Source: CAG (Commercial), GoI, 2007-08.

Categorisation

On the basis of the commodities and services these enterprises were dealt with, the SLPEs are classified into five categories, such as financial, manufacturing, promotional, utility and welfare enterprises. The number of enterprises functioning under each category is shown in Figure 1.2. The manufacturing and promotional enterprises constitute the largest number. The growth in the number of SLPEs and the increasing number of profit making units has increased the total investment levels. The investment was ₹ 4,4271.38 crore in 2006-07, which increased to ₹ 4,7813.29 crore in 2007-08. The investments were financed through the budgetary support from the state and central governments and other financial institutions.

Figure 1.2

Category-wise SLPEs

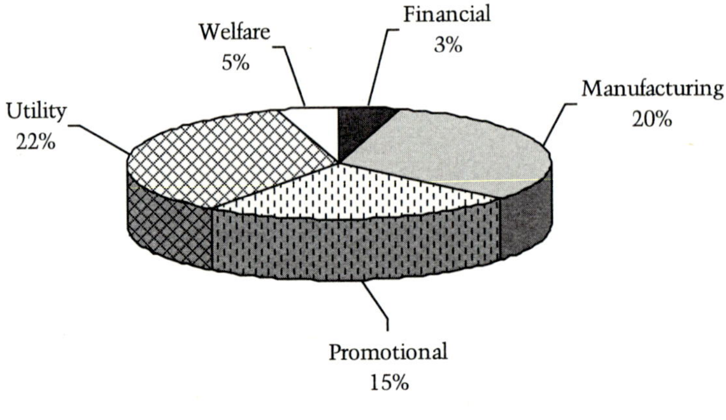

Source: CAG (Commercial), GoI and author's calculations.

Performance

The Government of Karnataka (GoK) is constantly reviewing the role of SLPEs in enhancing the financial performance, turnaround strategies, restoring discipline, realising full productivity, etc. Given the massive investment in the SLPEs, it is essential to examine the overall view of their performance. The sector-wise performance of SLPEs reveals that the enterprises in the financial and welfare sectors are running under losses or with high levels of government subsidy. The accumulated losses of the

SLPEs increased from ₹ 1,824.60 crore in 2006-07 to ₹ 2,148.31 crore in 2007-08, registering a growth of 15.1 per cent. Table 1.2 shows the sector-wise accumulated profits and losses of the SLPEs from 2005-06 to 2007-08.

Table 1.2

Accumulated Profit and Loss of SLPEs

(₹ in lakh)

No.	Particulars	2007-08	2006-07	2005-06
1.	Financial	-97257.3	-107804	5622.94
2.	Manufacturing	20875.29	3847.14	-10030.3
3.	Promotional	20731.45	21346.9	18204.95
4.	Utility	274014.5	268637.3	199787.2
5.	Welfare	-3532.57	-3567.98	-3018.46
	Total	214831	182460	210566

Source: CAG (Commercial), GoI, 2007-08.

Tables 1.3 and 1.4 present information on the top five profit and loss making units in Karnataka. Karnataka Power Corporation Limited, Hutti Gold Mines Company Limited and Bangalore Metropolitan Transport Corporation are ranked first, second and third, respectively, among the profit making SLPEs.

Table 1.3

Top Five Profit Making Units (2007-08)

(₹ in lakh)

No.	Name of the Enterprise	Amt
1.	Karnataka Power Corporation Limited	25022.67
2.	Hutti Gold Mines Company Limited	14489.81
3.	Bangalore Metropolitan Transport Corporation	14022.65
4.	Karnataka Power Transmission Corporation Limited	12488.15
5.	Mysore Minerals Limited	9820.03

Source: CAG (Commercial), GoI, 2007-08.

North Western Karnataka Road Transport Corporation (NWKRTC), Mysore Sugar Company Limited (MSCL) and Karnataka Road Development

Corporation Limited (KRDCL) are the major loss making units. KRDCL incurred loss owing to the inefficiency in the execution of the projects. MSCL was running in loss due to the non-availability of resources.

Table 1.4

Top Five Loss Making Units (2007-08)

(₹ in lakh)

No.	*Name of the Enterprise*	*Amt*
1.	North Western Karnataka Road Transport Corporation	6706.7
2.	Mysore Sugar Company Limited	2221.33
3.	Karnataka Road Development Corporation Limited	776.59
4.	Karnataka Land Army Corporation Limited	597.81
5.	Karnataka State Agro Corn Products Limited	441.92

Source: CAG (Commercial), GoI, 2007-08.

Thus, it can be summarised that both financial and welfare enterprises are loss-making sectors on an aggregated sense. On the other hand, the services sectors such as the promotional and the utilities sectors are performing well. According to the Public Enterprises Surveys and CAG reports of the GoI, because of the political interventions, bad managerial decisions, excessive employed manpower, etc., these organisations are not able to make profits. These surveys have shown that many enterprises in the financial and welfare sectors degenerated into chronic loss-making enterprises and which forced the state government of Karnataka to rethink its policies and measures towards the development of SLPEs in the state.

As far as the human resources are concerned, even after the initiation of the overall economic reforms in 1990-91, the growth rate of employment in the SLPEs that has been positive till 1994-95, started falling in 1997-98. It can be observed from the Figure 1.3 that the total employment in SLPEs fell over the years till 2005-06, but it has gone up from 1,56,480 in, 2005-06 to 1,68,811 in 2007-08. Most interestingly, the over-employment seems to be the major obstacle for the government's commitment to make the SLPEs competitive in the liberalised, privatised and globalised world.

Figure 1.3

Human Resources in SLPEs in Karnataka

Source: CAG (Commercial), GoI.

Budgetary Support

The data on budgetary support show a decline in the government support in terms of grants and subsidies to the SLPEs in 2007-08. Interestingly, the grants and subsidies given by the state and central government constitute the major share in the budget support followed by the equity. Table 1.5 shows the budgetary support of the SLPEs from 2005-06 to 2007-08.

Table 1.5

Budget Support to SLPEs (2006-2008)

(₹ in crore)

No.	Particulars	2005-06	2006-07	2007-08
1.	Equity	3248.34	2173.68	2610.65
2.	Loans	222.07	124.07	481.01
3.	Grants/subsidies	3008.99	6063.82	2252.79
4.	Total	6479.4	8361.57	5344.45

Source: CAG (Commercial), GoI, 2007-08.

The budgetary support to the SLPEs has been fluctuating over the years (Figure 1.4). The budgetary support increased from ₹ 6,479.4 crore in 2005-06 to ₹ 8,361.57 crore in 2006-07, registering a growth rate of 22.5 per cent. On the other hand, it has declined by 56 per cent in 2007-08. The point to be noted here is that usually the borrowings of the SLPEs are from the state government and when these enterprises fail to repay the loans, the government has to convert these loans into an investment. It has also been observed that the major reasons for the inability to repay the loans by these enterprises are deficiencies in financial management, lack of proper planning, lack of project implementation mechanism, lack of operations and monitoring capabilities.

Figure 1.4

Budgetary Support to SLPEs

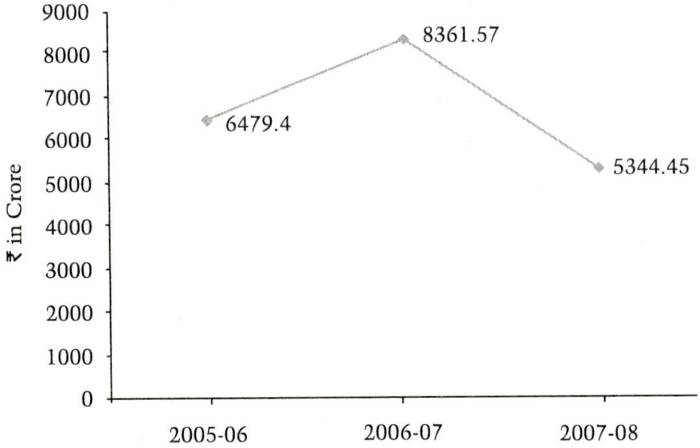

Source: CAG (Commercial), GoI, 2007-08.

Contribution to the State GDP

Karnataka occupies the first place in the country in terms of SLPEs with most of them making profits. Of the 65 SLPEs functioning in the state, more than 40 units are making profits and the enterprises that are making losses are 13 in number. SLPEs turnover to state GDP (SGDP) shows the extent of public enterprises activities in the state. Table 1.6 provides the details of SLPEs contribution to SGDP from 2005-06 to 2007-08.

Table 1.6

SLPEs Contribution to SGDP

(₹ in crore)

No.	Particulars	2005-06	2006-07	2007-08
1.	Turnover	28218.05	25284.7	21042.7
2.	State GDP	186209	200922	233802
3.	Percentage of Turnover to State GDP	15.15	12.58	9.00

Source: CAG (Commercial), GoI, 2007-08.

The percentage of turnover to the SGDP has been declining steadily over the years. Though there is an increase in the turnover of the manufacturing, promotional and utility sectors, their contribution to the SGDP has declined. The SLPEs can discharge their role efficiently, only if they are financially self-reliant. There is scope for improvement in overall performance, when the government introduces a performance-based system of accountability and imbibes greater degree of professionalism to ensure efficiency and profitability.

Government Reforms and Policy Initiatives

In 1980s, the state government of Karnataka initiated steps to improve the performance of SLPEs. As a first step towards the evaluation of the state government policies relating to these enterprises, the government formed a committee in August 1988 and another Cabinet sub-committee was formed in 1990, which recommended for privatisation of the loss making SLPEs in the state. But, due to the lack of proper implementation mechanism and political will, the recommendations of the sub-committee were not materialised. Again in March 2000, the government formed a Committee on "Public Sector Restructuring" with the following objectives:

- To evaluate the performance of SLPEs and suggest appropriate measures to promote greater productivity and profitability.
- To suggest measures to promote autonomy of SLPEs.
- To enable the government in identifying the enterprises that need state support or complete privatisation, those that need strategic

partners to reduce dependence on state budgetary support, those for which restructuring measures could be suggested, etc.

- To safeguard the interests of the human resources.

Memorandum of Understanding (MoU) was introduced with a vision to know the performance of SLPEs. The MoU mentions self-imposed physical and financial targets for coming three years and promises made to the government about enhancement of performance. This created competition among the SLPEs and the private sector. The SLPEs were encouraged, restructured and amalgamated to become prosperous, healthy and efficient vehicles, surging forward delivery of developed assets to the people, the nation, so that the state becomes prosperous and self-reliant.

Conclusion

The GoK is continuously reviewing the role and performance of the PSEs from various aspects. The most important are states presence in any sector of public service like utilities, welfare, etc.; advances in technology; new realities of pricing and marketing strategies; issues in human resource management, etc. It has also been realised that whatever the sectors, manufacturing, welfare, financial or utilities, the ultimate performance can be judged by their ability to sustain in the globally competitive world and to generate their own resources for growth. In the past, SLPEs used to come before government only with grievances and problems. Now, there is a change in trend i.e., SLPEs are coming before the government with good performance, so that they could be awarded and rewarded.

2 Hutti Gold Mines Limited

Lakshmi Kumari and
S.S. Subrahmanyam

Origin and Objectives

The Hutti Gold Mines Company Ltd. (HGML), a state public sector enterprise undertaking, came into existence with the prime objective of producing gold and to carry out exploration activities to increase the ore reserves of the mining areas and find new deposits of gold. The company entered into MoU (Memorandum of Understanding) with Department of Public Enterprises (DPE), Government of Karnataka (GoK), setting out the vision, mission and objectives along with parameters for monitoring and evaluating the performance of the company.

Vision

- Improve productivity and profitability.
- Provide financial stability on long term.
- Register steady growth in terms of percentage of capacity utilisation, production, income and overall profitability.
- Provide safe working condition in the mine.
- Introduction of modern and effective management control systems.
- Give more importance to the mine development apart from achieving day-to-day production target.
- Promote harmonious and cordial industrial relationship.
- Promote human resource development.
- Promote welfare and community development in Hutti village.

- Have environment friendly and healthy mining and production process.
- Have good health and well-being of workers staff and employees.

Objectives

- To carry out exploration activities to increase the ore reserves of the mining areas and find new deposits.
- To beneficiate, smelt, refine, cast of finished gold metal into salable products in the form of bullion buttons.
- To increase the efficiency of mines and plants with the cost reduction by producing 2,000 tonnes per day, by implementing the modernisation/expansion project.
- To improve profitability.
- To achieve financial stability.
- To achieve the targets and goals set by the board.
- To undertake appropriate pollution control measures and to improve the standards of safety.
- To undertake measures for improving the quality of social life of employee.

Mission

- The company is mainly engaged in the mining of gold at Hutti and Chitradurga.
- To develop HGML industry on sound lines by exploiting existing gold deposits and developing new gold deposits located in various parts of Karnataka.
- Adoption of appropriate cost-effective measures.
- Introduction of modern technology in order to maximise indigenous production of gold.
- It is aimed to make the company self-reliant and financially viable to increase production.

Corporate Social Responsibility

Under corporate social responsibility, the company is taking care of environmental protection, social welfare and health care operations.

Environment and Energy Conservation

Company's policy of conservation of natural resources by judicious consumption continues. An Environment Cell has been formed to continuously monitor the activities. Afforestation has been taken up in the vacant areas and area surrounding the tailings dump. Every year plantation is being done in and around the plant and avenue areas in consultation with local forest department. Mill tailings are detoxified before sending to tailings dump and the company has also introduced high rate thickener in detoxification plant to help reclaim water containing cyanide and reduce fresh water consumption and thus facilitating conservation of water. In addition to this, the domestic effluents are treated and the discharged water is recycled for plantation. Water samples from the surrounding areas are drawn periodically and sent for analysis. Regular monitoring of ambient air, water and noise levels are done to control the pollution of environment. To conserve electricity/fuel, solar water heaters and lightings are being proposed.

Social Welfare and Health Care (HGM Hospital)

The Hutti Gold Mines has a full-fledged 120-bedded hospital, catering to the needs of about 4,000 company employees and their dependents. Besides, it also treats out-patients from neighbouring villages at nominal charges. At present 20 doctors comprising specialists and non-specialists along with 125 para medical personnel are working in the hospital. The daily out-patients range from 850-1000. About 1,89,733 out-patients and 23,333 in-patients were treated in the company hospital during the year 2008-09. Further, around 1,969 operations were conducted in the hospital during the year 2008-09.

Amenities and Welfare

Alive to the social responsibilities to the communities in which it operates, the company provides various welfare amenities, such as residential accommodation, medical facilities, cooperative stores, educational facilities, growth of forestry and environment, as well as other facilities like subsidised canteen, drinking water, power supply, play grounds, community centre, etc. HGML has also erected dish antennae on the campus for viewing television in residences and community centres. Banking, postal and cooperative society facilities have also been provided. Various tournaments are organised from time to time.

Waste Disposal

The barren pulp from carbon in pulp (CIP) is subjected to classification in a battery of hydro cyclone, and coarse sand thus generated is used in mines for back filling purpose. The cyclones overflow (fines) is sent to high rate tailing thickener to reclaim the water, and thickener underflow is subjected to detoxification in a series of mechanical agitators with the help of bleaching powder. The barren and detoxified pulp is disposed off to tailing dam. The reclaimed water from tailing dump is pumped to the processing plant and thus, zero discharge is maintained. Environmental management at HGML follows standard environmental management plans and pollution control measures as per guidelines laid down by statutory bodies. HGML has a well-established environmental laboratory for monitoring and implementing environmental management plans, and has relevant research & development (R&D) to maintain the eco-friendly environment.

Education

The company periodically organises training programmes for its employees and officers. Classes for staff and workers are being organised on a regular basis. Merit awards are given to the children of employees, excelling in examinations. The Board of Directors have approved payment of ₹ 5 lakh as contribution for construction of Mathematics laboratory which also received support from Science Centre, Raichur.

Production and Operating Results

5,70,447 MT of ore was treated during 2008-09, against 5,62,921 MT in 2007-08. The company hoisted 5,04,654 MT of ore during the year 2008-09 as against 5,01,640 MT in the year 2007-08. The ore transported from UT open cast mine and Hirabuddini gold unit was 57,267 MT and

9,219 MT during the year 2008-09 as against 52,086 MT and 13,258 MT during the year 2007-08.

Phase II Mining

Hutti Mine has established infrastructure like rock breaker at 20th level, underground crusher and a speed winder exclusively for continuous ore histing from 24th level to cater the ore reserves blocked from 20th level and above. In order to sustain continuous run-of-mine (ROM) grade of 5 gm/tonne and to blend low grade ore with available high grade blocks above 20th level for mining, second phase of mining activity below 20th level has been commenced from December 2008. Although considerable amount of ore reserves are blocked below 20th level to 24th level, the similar existing infrastructure like rock breaker, U/G crusher and loading system is planned by deepening mallappa shaft up to 28th level and later to connect to new shaft. The existing shaft winze in ZI reef has reached up to the roof of planned underground crusher i.e., at 27th level which will be later converted to OTR. Initially two stopes are being prepared for future production in ZI reef between 22nd level to 24th level.

New Ball and Sag Mill

A new ball and sag mill scheduled to commence from November 2009 plans to feed the new mill @200 tpd (tonnes per day). The break-up tpd to mill is given as follows:

Hutti Mine	1480 MT
UTI Gold Mine	400 MT
HB GM	120 MT
Total	2000TPD

Load Haul and Dump (LHD)

Existing M#LHD is planned to re-locate from SRF 12th level below JE34 to SR 11th level GE32 wide ore body region. Two 0.9 M3 remote controlled LHDs are planned during 2009-10 to be deployed at SRF 12th level below JE 34 and at ZI 17 below CE35 region; all preparatory work is in progress.

Ore Handling System

At MS 20th level main haulage cross-cut east to SR OTR, the main track line is upgraded with 0 lbs rails; from 40 lbs it is planned to have two independent tracks up to the rock breaker to handle the ore dumped, about 500-600 TPD in the OTR.

Grey Shaft

Exploratory mine development by the contractor M/s TCL has started at 4th and 64th level, while developing at 4th level, 8 mtrs width of the ore body has been established for a strike length of about 200 mts at an average grade of 2.8 to 3 gm/tonne, it appears that southern portion of main mine has potential for future mining in Hutti area.

South Hutti

Low grade stope is being prepared from 1st and 3rd level. The width of the ore body has proved in some places up to 11 mtrs for a strike length of about 100 mts. The low grade stope will come into production, once the contractor hands over the site for mining.

Sand Stowing

2,20,948 MT of classified tailing was stowed in U/G stope voids in the year 2008-09 against 2,32,820 MT in the previous year 2007-08.

Ventilation

Booster fan which is installed at MS 24th level is working satisfactorily, catering ZI & strike reef workings. The other booster fan at middle reef at 20th level needs to be relocated from GE 51 to GE 52 region, as MR20 sub-level stope GE51 is planned to bring into production from mid 2009-10.

UTI Gold Unit (Open Pit Mine)

The open-pit mining (Phase-III) work was in progress. The operational ratios explain:

- Utilising the business assets optimally by balancing productivity and maintenance.

- Training and motivating employees to make them equipped and willing to play their roles competently.
- Managing inventories, receivables and production operations to speed up the throughput of funds.
- Good performance in these areas determines how successfully a company is building up shareholder value.

Major Performance Ratios

Fixed Assets Turnover Ratio

Fixed Assets Turnover Ratio = Revenue/Property, Plant and Equipment

Fixed assets of a business are the facilities needed to earn its revenues. The fixed asset turnover ratio computes how many times the outlay on these facilities have been covered by the revenues earned. The higher the turnover, the better the performance, indicating effective utilisation of the assets, and also avoiding unnecessary investment in facilities. Looking at it in another way, fixed assets turnover ratio measures, how well the company's investment decisions turned out.

Table 2.1

Fixed Assets Turnover Ratio Measures Company's Investment

Years	*Sales*	*GFA*	*Ratio*
2002-03	14332.75	8190.53	1.75
2003-04	17340.45	8391.78	2.07
2004-05	18059.78	8637.33	2.09
2005-06	20715.62	8984.99	2.31
2006-07	22071.83	9236.91	2.39
2007-08	30351.35	12843.64	2.36
2008-09	31602.79	16974.44	1.86

Source: Compiled from Annual Reports.

For one rupee of investment, the sales are at 1.75. There is not much of increase in sales to investment.

Sales Performance Ratio

Sales Revenue Per Employee = *Revenue/Average Number of Employees During the Period*

The per employee sales performance ratio measures revenue productivity, which is affected by employee selection, training, working environment and motivation. All decisions and activities of a company are carried out by individual employees and sales performance ratio focuses attention on this aspect.

Figure 2.1

Sales to Investment Ratio

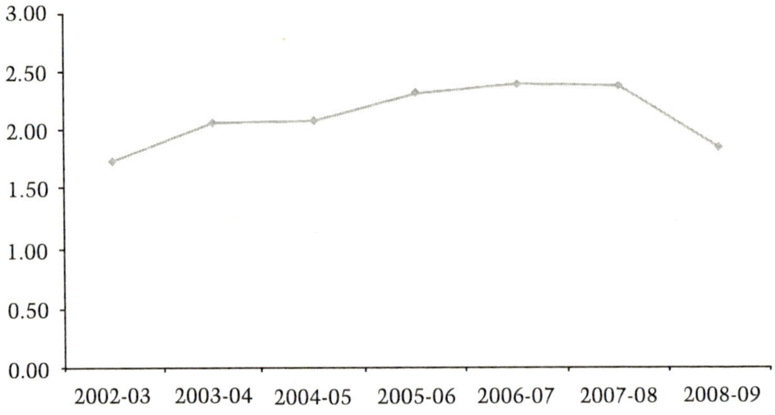

Source: Compiled from Annual Reports.

Table 2.2

Employees Sales Performance

Years	*No. of Employees*	*Sales*	*Sales/Number*
2002-03	4128.00	14332.75	3.47
2003-04	4030.00	17340.45	4.30
2004-05	4096.00	18059.78	4.41
2005-06	4078	20715.62	5.08
2006-07	4031	22071.83	5.48
2007-08	3959	30351.35	7.67
2008-09	3933	31602.79	8.04

Source: Compiled from Annual Reports.

Figure 2.2

Employees Sales Performance Ratios

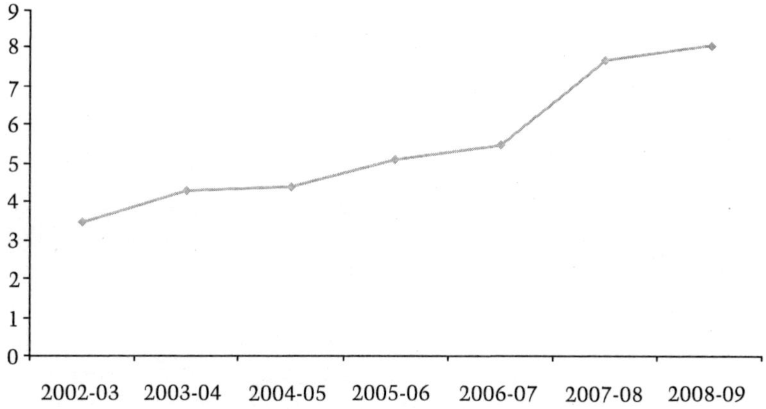

Source: Compiled from Annual Reports.

Financial Performance

During 2008-09, the value of production amounted to ₹ 31,340 lakh as against ₹ 28,632 lakh, an increase of 9.46 per cent over 2007-08.

Capital Structure

As at the close of March 31, 2008, the paid-up capital of the corporation stood at ₹ 296.20 lakh.

Reserves and Surplus

The reserves and surplus accumulated upto March 31, 2009 was ₹ 36,133.26 lakh as against ₹ 29,240.97 lakh as on March 31, 2008.

Net Profit: The company net profit showed a remarkable progress over the years 2002-03 to 2008-09. During the year 2009-10, ₹ 15,396 lakh as against ₹ 14,494 lakh during the year 2008-09. The year 2007-08 is a breakthrough in the performance of the company, which experienced a drastic jump in the net profit. This is clearly explained with the help of Figure 2.3.

Tables 2.3

Financial Parameter

(₹ in lakh)

Particulars	*2002-03*	*2003-04*	*2004-05*	*2005-06*	*2006-07*	*2007-08*	*2008-09*
Paid-up capital	296	296	296	296	296	296	296
Reserves and Surplus	1977	4884	9167	14775	19956	29241	36133
Borrowings	3827	3003	1210	702	1295	542	0
Deferred Tax Liability (net)	95	589	809	947	1340	1713	2219
Current Liabilities and Provisions	4274	4832	5867	8936	13200	13711	20937
Total	10470	13604	17349	25656	36087	45503	59585
Net Fixed Assets	5281	5187	5288	7175	8843	12797	18087
Investment	0	1677	2265	4895	7767	4368	1570
Total Income	14333	17340	19436	21048	23356	32220	34132
Sales	13232	16342	18060	20715	22164	30351	31603
Net Profit	2289	4856	7324	8193	8528	14494	15396
Current Loans and Advances	3307	5167	8710	12849	17983	27256	39698
Miscellaneous Expenditure	1882	1573	1086	737	1494	1082	230

Source: Compiled from Annual Reports.

Figure 2.3

Net Profit

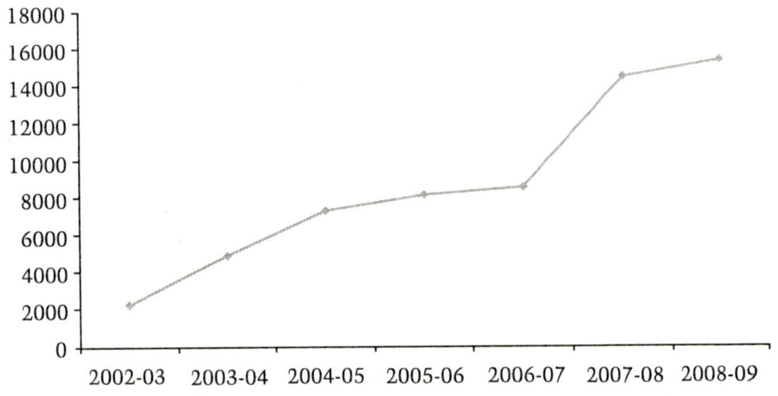

Source: Compiled from Annual Reports.

Figure 2.4

Sales

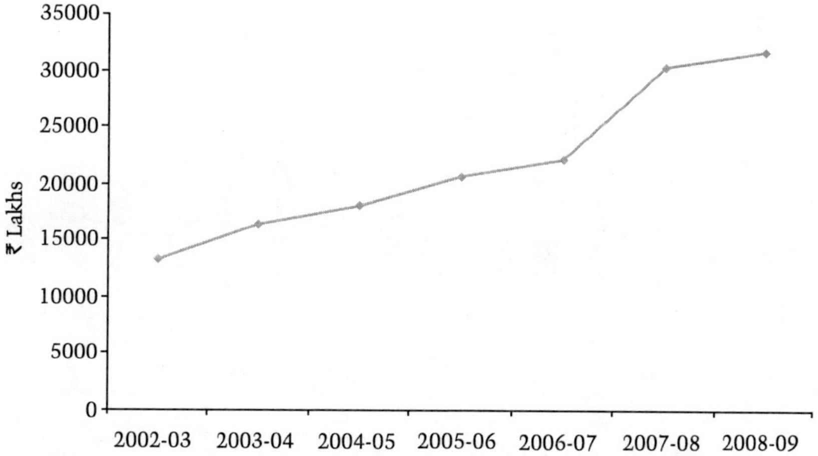

Source: Compiled from Annual Reports.

Table 2.4

Physical Performance

Year	*Ore Treated (MT)*	*Gold Produced (Kg)*
1995-96	232626	1011.09
1996-97	283083	1594.16
1997-98	293640	1648.69
1998-99	323974	1647.46
1999-2000	349084	1580.48
2000-01	335845	1958.47
2001-02	409437	2416.33
2002-03	525928	2709.00
2003-04	573577	3107.77
2004-05	592685	3507.61
2005-06	513722	2848.34
2006-07	522374	2336.27
2007-08	562921	2808.38
2008-09	570447	2420.38

Source: Compiled from Annual Reports.

Figure 2.5

Gold Produced

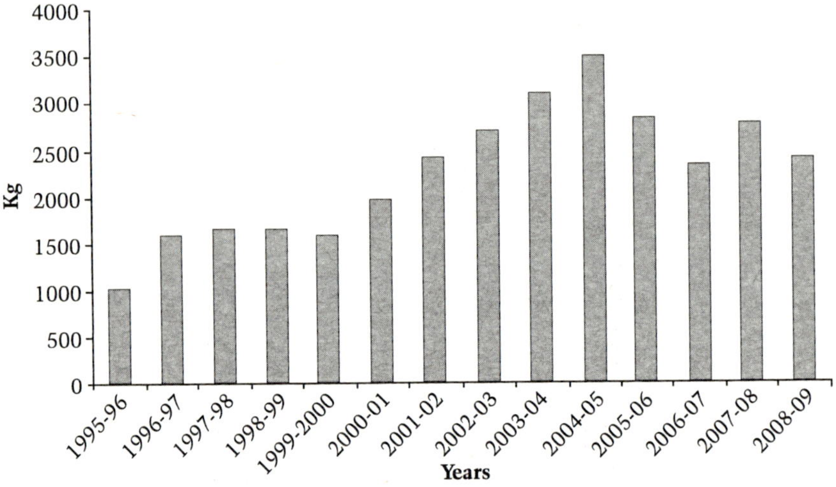

Source: Compiled from Annual Reports.

Financial Performance Evaluation of Hutti Gold Mines

Ratio analysis is a powerful tool of financial analysis. A ratio is defined as "the indicated quotient of two mathematical expressions" and as "the relationship between two or more things." In financial analysis, a ratio is used as a benchmark for evaluating the financial position and performance of a corporation. The absolute accounting figures reported in the financial statement do not provide a meaningful understanding of the performance and financial position of a corporation. An accounting figure conveys meaning, when it is related to some other relevant information. For example, a ₹ 5 crore net profit may look impressive but the firm's performance can said to be good or bad only when the net profit figure is related to the corporation's investment. The relationship between two accounting figures, expressed mathematically, is known as a financial ratio. Ratios help to summarise large quantities of financial data and to make qualitative judgement about the corporation's financial performance. For instance, consider current ratio. It is calculated by dividing current assets by current liabilities; the ratio indicates a relationship—a quantified relationship—between current assets and current liabilities. This relationship is an index or yardstick, which permits a qualitative judgement to be formed about the corporation's ability to meet its current obligations. It measures the corporation's liquidity. The greater the ratio, the greater the firm's liquidity and *vice versa*. The point to note is that a ratio reflecting a quantitative relationship helps to form a qualitative judgement. Such is the nature of all financial ratios.

Several ratios, calculated from the accounting data, can be grouped into various classes according to financial activity or function to be evaluated. The parties interested in financial analysis are short- and long-term creditors, owners and management. Short-term creditors' main interest is in the liquidity position or the short-term solvency of the corporation. Long-term creditors, on the other hand, are more interested in the long-term solvency and profitability of the corporation. Similarly, owners concentrate on the corporation's profitability and financial condition. Management is interested in evaluating every aspect of the corporation's performance. They have to protect the interests of all parties and see that the corporation grows profitably. In view of the requirements of the various users of ratios, the ratios are classified into the following three categories:

- Liquidity Ratios.
- Leverage Ratios.
- Profitability Ratios.

Liquidity Ratios

Liquidity ratios measure the corporation's ability to meet current obligations. The two ratios under liquidity ratios *viz.*, current ratio and quick ratio are analysed here. The current ratio is a measure of the corporate short-term solvency. It indicates the availability of current assets in rupees for every one rupee of current liability. A ratio greater than one means that the corporation has more current assets than current liabilities. During the years 2002-03 and 2008-09 the entire study period, the company had more current assets and it was not involved in liabilities trap.

Quick ratio establishes a relationship between liquid assets and current liabilities. If the ratio is less than one, then it is easy to convert quick assets into liquid form to meet its obligations. Here, in case of this company, the quick ratio during the period was on an average 0.99, which represents a satisfactory current financial condition. This is clearly explained with the help of Figure 2.6.

Table 2.5

Quick Ratio Establishes a Relationship between Liquid Assets and Current Liabilities

Years	*Current Assets*	*Current Liabilities*	*Current Ratio*	*Quick Ratio*
2002-03	3306.87	4274.38	0.77	0.40
2003-04	5166.62	4832.23	1.07	0.49
2004-05	8710.39	5867.44	1.48	0.85
2005-06	12849.07	8939.72	1.44	1.00
2006-07	17982.75	13199.71	1.36	0.99
2007-08	27256.41	13711.05	1.99	1.62
2008-09	39697.75	20937.43	1.90	1.62

Source: Compiled from Annual Reports.

Figure 2.6

Liquidity Ratios

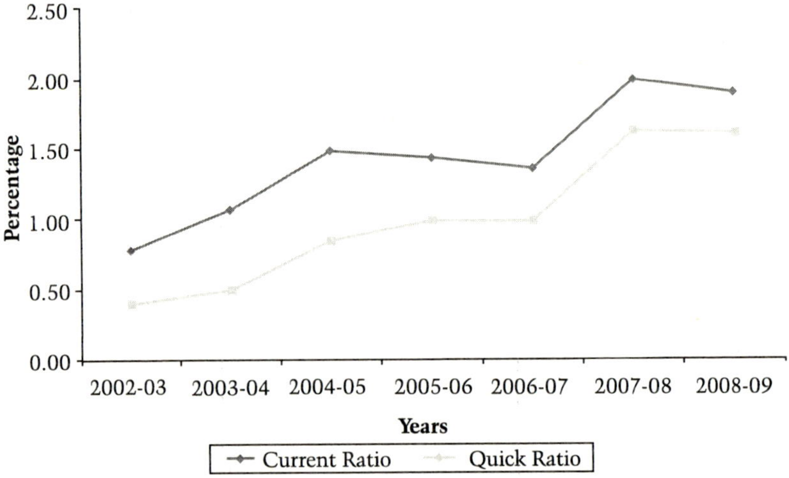

Source: Compiled from Annual Reports.

Leverage Ratios

Leverage ratios show the proportions of debt and equity in financing the firm's assets. It is clear from Figure 2.7 that the lenders contribution is less than one rupee, if the owners contribution is one rupee. It is only during the years 2004-05 to 2006-07 that the lenders contribution was more than one rupee of owner's contribution. Debt equity ratio is directly computed by dividing total debt by net worth. The debt equity ratio of the company moved from 12.9:1 in 2002-03 to 1.82:1 in 2008-09, which shows that the company is managing more on equity rather than on debt, thus a healthy improvement of the performance in recent years.

Figure 2.7

Debt Equity Ratios

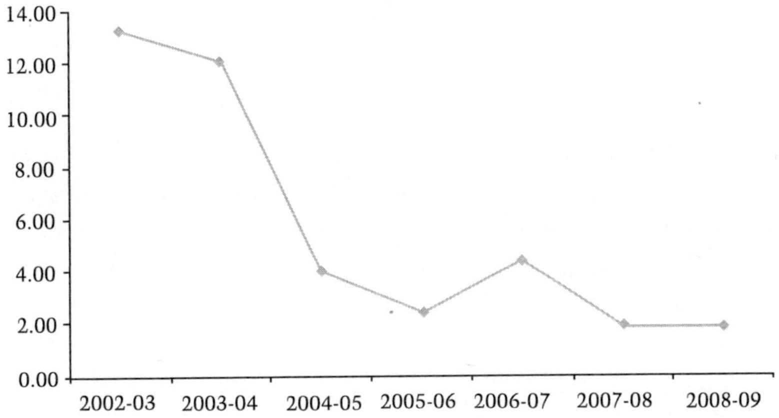

Source: Compiled from Annual Reports.

Profitability Ratios

A corporation should earn profits to survive and grow over a long period of time. Profits are essential but it would be wrong to assume that every action initiated by management of a company should be aimed at maximising profits, irrespective of concerns for customers, employees, suppliers or social consequcnces. It is unfortunate that the word 'profit' is looked upon as a term of abuse since some corporations always want to maximise profits at the cost of employees, customers and society. Except such infrequent cases, it is a fact that sufficient profits must be earned to sustain the operations of the business to be able to obtain funds from investors for expansion and growth, and to contribute towards the social overheads for the welfare of the society.

Profit is the difference between revenues and expenses over a period of time. Profit is the ultimate 'output' of a corporation, and it will have no future if it fails to make sufficient profits. Therefore, the financial manager should continuously evaluate the efficiency of the company in terms of profits. The profitability ratios are calculated to measure the operating efficiency of the company in terms of profits. Generally, two types of profitability ratios are calculated:

- Profitability in relation to sales.
- Profitability in relation to investment.

Return on Sales (ROS) Ratio

This ratio is widely used to evaluate an enterprises operational efficiency. ROS is also known as a firm's 'operating profit margin.' It is calculated using the formula, 'Profit Before Depreciation, Interest and Taxes/Sales.' This measure is helpful to management and provides an insight into how much profit is being produced per rupee of sales. As with many ratios, it is best to compare the enterprise's ROS over time to look for trends, and also compare it with similar public enterprises. An increasing ROS indicates the enterprise is growing more efficient, while a decreasing ROS could signal looming financial troubles. This decrease in ROS was experienced by the corporation during the year 2004-05 to 2006-07, but in recent years the company experienced a good return on sales.

Figure 2.8

Return on Sales (ROS) Ratio

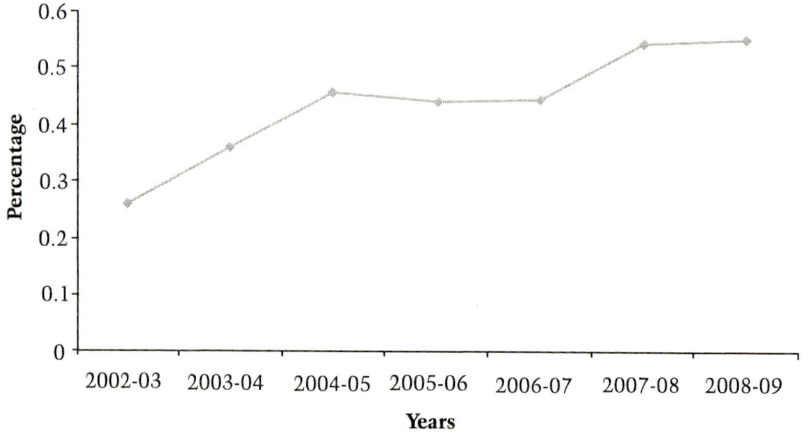

Source: Compiled from Annual Reports.

Return on Assets (ROA) Ratio

ROA is an indicator of how profitable an enterprise is relative to its total assets. ROA gives an idea as to how efficient management is at using its assets to generate earnings. Calculated by dividing an enterprise's annual earnings by its total assets, ROA is displayed as a percentage. Sometimes this is referred to as 'return on investment.' ROA explains the earnings that is generated from invested capital (assets). ROA for public companies can vary substantially and is highly dependent on the industry. This is why, when using ROA as a comparative measure, it is best to compare it against the enterprise's previous ROA numbers or the ROA of a similar enterprise. The assets of the enterprise are comprised both debt and equity. Both of these types of financing are used to fund the operations of the enterprise. The ROA figure gives investors an idea of how effectively the enterprise is converting the money, it has to invest into net income. The higher the ROA, the better because, the enterprise is earning more money on less investment. This ROA of the enterprises is highest during the year 2004-05. The years 2005-06 to 2006-07 experienced a drastic fall and after 2007-08, the company slowly improved its performance.

Figure 2.9

Return on Assets (ROA) Ratio

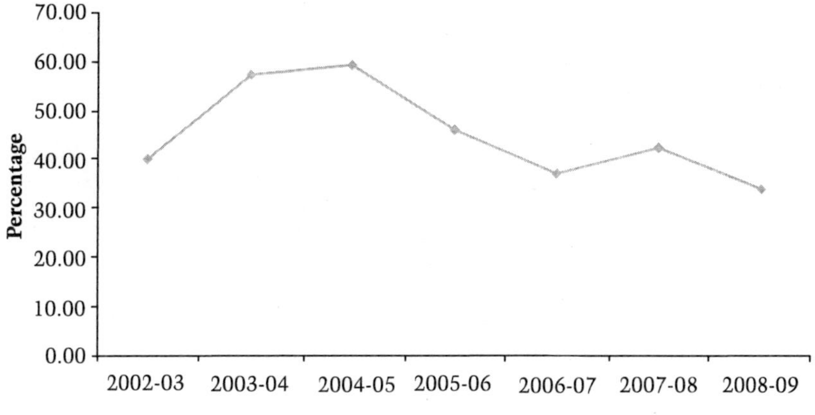

Source: Compiled from Annual Reports.

Return on Equity (ROE) Ratio

ROE is a measure of the profitability that reveals how much profit the enterprise is generating with the money that shareholders have invested. ROE is useful for comparing the profitability of an enterprise with that of other firms, in the same industry. Figure 2.10 shows that the return on equity is at its highest during the year 2007-08 and has experienced a steady progress over the years.

Figure 2.10

Return on Equity

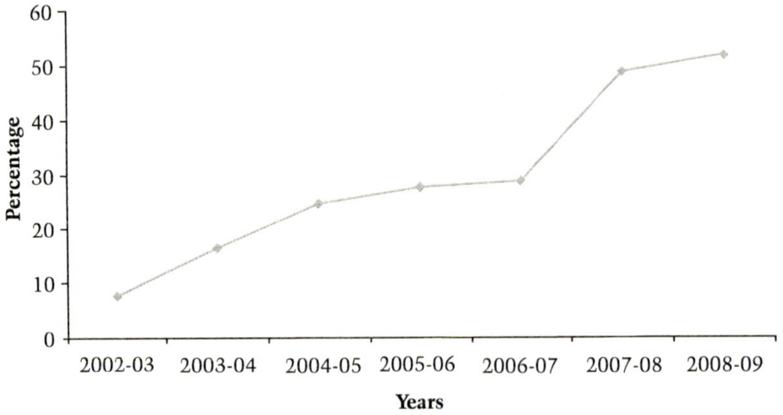

Source: Compiled from Annual Reports.

Table 2.6

Profitability Ratios

Years	*ROS*	*ROI*	*ROE*
2002-03	0.26	40.06	7.73
2003-04	0.36	56.98	16.41
2004-05	0.46	59.10	24.74
2005-06	0.44	45.85	27.68
2006-07	0.45	37.00	28.81
2007-08	0.54	42.40	48.97
2008-09	0.55	34.00	52.01

Source: Compiled from Annual Reports.

Findings, Summary and Recommendations

- The company had entered into MoU with DPE, Government of Karnataka, for the years 2009-10 to 2011-12 with the prime objective of producing gold and to carry out exploration activities to utilise the ore reserves and also to find out availability of new deposits of gold.
- The company could fulfill its set targets up to 70 per cent in the current year of operations. The main reason being, the availability of low grade gold in the ore deposits.
- The company is presently (as of January 27, 2010) carrying operations at a depth of 2,000 feet from the surface level and is intending to go beyond 2,500 to 3,000 feet vertically.
- The company has made all the possibilities to go horizontally to find out improvised ore deposits (i.e., for better grade). However, when the company tried to extend their operations horizontally, especially north side, they could not penetrate further, due to non-availability of mining lease. It has been understood that the leasing rights have been given to private parties. Hence, it is recommended that government shall make all possible arrangements for getting mining leases on the name of the company.
- The employee strength as of now is 4,100, including all cadres of workmen. This may go up at the rate of 10-15 per cent, if the above point is fulfilled.
- It has been noticed that the turn-out ratio is about 8-10 per cent overall. However, it has been observed that this ratio is slightly high in the area of mining and processing. In addition, the department is headed by a deputy general manager. Hence, it is proposed that it shall be headed by a general manager with suitable technical qualifications and experience.
- It has been observed that the company is loosing its skilled human resources, mainly due to wage parity. It is also noticed that the company's wage structure is lower than Karnataka Power Transmission Corporation (KPTCL) Ltd., a state-owned public

sector. Since mining is a risk pruned activity and also many people are leaving to central sectors like National Mineral Development Corporation (NMDC) etc., due high emoluments, government could think of solving this problem i.e., mainly for retaining. If not in direct wage, some risk allowances may be provided to compensate this parity problem.

- The company is providing a lot of incentives in the form of food kit allowance, attendance bonus, yearly bonus, LTC, etc., to motivate all the employees besides other general formalities as per the company's act.
- It has also been understood that the company is implementing four schemes for the employees to take care of their livelihood, even after retirement.
- It has been observed the waste is containing around 0.3 grams of gold per tonne of raw material. Hence, it is proposed that a study shall be made in detail to recover at least part of the remaining gold. This problem may be discussed with prominent research institutes like Indian Institute of Chemical Technology (IICT), Hyderabad, or Defence Metallurgical Research Laboratories (DMRL), Hyderabad, or National Geophysical Research Institute (NGRI) or any other suitable institute for better improvement and solving the problem.
- The company has made considerable contribution to the state exchequer in the form of dividend payments. The details of the same are as follows:

Table 2.7

Dividend Payment

Year	*Equity owned by Government (₹ in Lakh)*	*Dividend payment in per cent of Equity*
2008-09	248	200
2007-08	-do-	100
2006-07	-do-	100
2005-06	-do-	50

Source: Compiled from Annual Reports.

From the above, it can be seen that the performance has improved. The company has also made substantial profits during the above years (may be due price escalation in the market).

- The company has also contributed in the form of corporate social responsibility in the form of constructing houses and distributing aid to the poor in the areas effected by recent floods. The construction of houses will be carried out on the basis of identification and recommendation of respective district collectors. This is in addition to helping the effected personnel at the time of actual floods by distributing food packets, clothes, water, etc. This project is estimated to cost around ₹ 10 crore to the company.
- The company is also running 125 bed hospital to take care of emergency and general medical needs of the employees. However, the authorities are facing problems in sustaining the experts in the concerned fields like gynecology, cardiology, radiology and general physicians, to cater the needs of the employees. Presently, the concerned employees requiring these services (in case of non-availability) are being deputed to the nearby hospitals, wherever the facility is available. Hence, it is requested that the government shall take a positive view on the problem in deputing suitable personnel, though not fully but at least to the partial extent.
- It is observed that the company is going for replacement of old machinery with new Sag & Ball Mill for improving the performance at two sections. The project cost is estimated at ₹ 63.44 crore. This will improve the performance by cutting down the unproductive timings to certain extent. However, it is recommended that that an alternative refinery section also be added for further improvement. Since all the tanks have become old, their life also has been diminished. If possible, method study for complete process shall be carried out for improving productivity of the overall plant.
- It is noticed that enterprise resource programmes (ERP) are being carried out at certain work centres. For better understanding of the functions and package, it is recommended that suitable personnel

from the concerned departments may be trained to get hands on experience and also to be aware of the situations. Especially, finance is one area, which requires high awareness of the system to be followed.

3 Karnataka Power Transmission Corporation Limited

S.S. Subrahmanyam

Introduction

Karnataka Power Transmission Corporation Limited (KPTCL), a registered company under the Companies Act, 1956, was incorporated on July 28, 1999 and is a company wholly owned by Government of Karnataka (GoK) with an authorised share capital of ₹ 1,000 crore. KPTCL was formed on August 1, 1999, by carving out the transmission and distribution (T&D) functions of the erstwhile Karnataka Electricity Board. KPTCL is headed by a chairman and managing director (CMD) at the corporate office. The CMD is assisted by four functional directors. The board of KPTCL consists of a maximum of 12 directors. KPTCL is mainly vested with the functions of T&D of power in the entire state of Karnataka. It operates under a license issued by Karnataka Electricity Regulatory Commission. KPTCL purchases power from Karnataka Power Corporation Limited which generates and operates major power generating projects in the state, consisting of hydel, thermal and other sources. KPTCL purchases power from KPCL at the rate fixed by the state government from time to time. KPTCL also purchases power from central-government-owned generating stations like National Thermal Power Corporation (NTPC), Neyvelli Lignite Corporation and the Atomic Power Stations at Kalpakkam and Kaiga. The approximate share of power from these generating stations is around 16 per cent. KPTCL serves nearly 146 lakh consumers of different categories spread all over the state, covering an area of 1.92 lakh square kms. To transmit and distribute power in the state, it operates nearly 684 sub-stations, 28,000 kms of transmission lines with voltages of 33 KV and above, nearly 1,30,000 kms of 11 KV lines, 1,50,000 distribution transformers and 3,57,000 kms of LT lines. One rural electric cooperative society is functioning in Hukkeri *taluka*, Belgaum district, which purchases bulk power from KPTCL and redistributes it to the consumers within the *taluka*. To enable easier operation of the system, KPTCL has been divided into 5 zones, each headed by a chief engineer; 15 circles, each headed by a superintending engineer; 57 divisions, each headed by an executive engineer; and over 270 sub-divisions, each headed by an assistant executive engineer. Maintenance of power supply and day-to-day functioning are being looked after by the above officers.

Vision and Mission

The mission of KPTCL is to ensure reliable quality power to its customers at competitive prices. The KPTCL is committed to achieve this mission through:

- Encouraging best practices in transmission and distribution.
- Ensuring high order maintenance of all its technical facilities.
- Emphasising the best standards in customer service.

Manpower

Human resources are regarded as one of the most significant asset of the organisation. Towards improving their skill sets, focus is given to proper training and orientation. The focus area of training and development of personnel at HRD centre, KPTCL, is follows:

Induction and Orientation Programme

The objectives of these programmes are to impart knowledge of the organisation, its business, its customers and its philosophy, value system, etc., to the newly recruited employees. The following programmes are conducted under this category:

- Pre-employment training to overseers/meter readers/operators/ store keepers/assistant store keepers, *daftharies*, junior assistants and assistants.
- Pre-employment training to assistant engineers (AEs)/junior engineers (JEs).

- Induction programme to the newly recruited probationary assistant accounts officers (AAOs).
- Orientation programme for AE/JE appointed on contract basis.
- Orientation programme for the newly promoted AAOs.

So far, 563 employees of Group B and C & D employees have undergone this training.

Training for Promotions

The training for promotions is designed to enable employees to move up the corporate ladder. The recruitment and promotion rules of the organisation provide opportunity to the employees to move to a higher cadre, after passing the prescribed examination. The following programmes are conducted under this category:

- Pre-promotion training to maintenance staff to be promoted as overseers/meter readers/operators/store keepers/assistant store keepers to be promoted as JEs.
- Training for change of cadre from *mali*/watchman to assistant lineman.
- Special coaching for scheduled caste/scheduled tribe (SC/ST) employees to appear for SAS (Subordinate Account Service) examination and to be promoted as AAOs.

So far, 99 employees of Group C & D have undergone this training.

Functional Training

This training is designed as on-the-job training, specific to the role the employee has been assigned. Here, the employee is taken through the workflow and expectations from each position. Generic programmes on topics such as safety at the work place, quality standards, etc., are also covered under this programme. The following programmes are conducted under this category:

- Orientation programme for candidates passing SAS and promoted as AAOs.
- Refresher courses for all cadres.

- Residential programme for senior officers on management aspects.
- Deputation of officers to various training programmes conducted by reputed institutions.

So far, 102 employees of Group A, B and C & D have undergone this training.

Behavioural (Personality Development) Training

This training field covers a wide gamut of skills, including positive attitude, communication, motivation, delegation and leadership. It also includes increasingly important subjects such as cross-cultural sensitivity and etiquette, team building and stress management. The results of behavioural training are difficult to measure but easy to perceive as such results cannot be qualified as clearly as other initiatives. HRD centre has embarked upon behavioural training by suitably designing all aspects of soft skills in one programme called "Personality Development Programme."

Physical Performance

To make an in-depth study about the organisation in order to realise the financial and physical performance of the organisation and to know the strengths of the organisation in the coming years, various financial and operational measurements of the company were made. KPTCL plays a significant role in the power sector of the state. It is the most important link between the generators and distribution companies. KPTCL has undergone a sea change in the last decade and is all set to undergo a paradigm shift in the next few years. Unbundling of the sector has resulted in five regional distribution companies (Electricity Supply Company [ESCOM]: BESCOM, MESCOM, GESCOM, HESCOM and CESC), and the lone transmission company (KPTCL). Trading has been delinked from the transmission company and the responsibility now vests with the respective (ESCOMs). The Electricity Act, 2003, provides a lot of scope for bringing a radical change in the sector. The regulatory regime in the state is in full force and has initiated several measures to bring the intended change in the sector. Open access has been introduced, which provides for the issue of license to procure power as open access customer. Transmission function in the state has improved to a great extent. The transmission loss has been provisionally worked out at 4.3 per cent, which matches the best anywhere across the globe. Unlike distribution, transmission requires huge investments to expand the network, overcome the constraints and to maintain the current levels of performance. The power sector is unique in the sense that it has to meet the demands of all the sectors of the society *viz.*, industry, agriculture, common man, socially and economically weaker sectors, etc.; it concerns every one, everywhere and anytime.

Figure 3.1

Transmission Losses

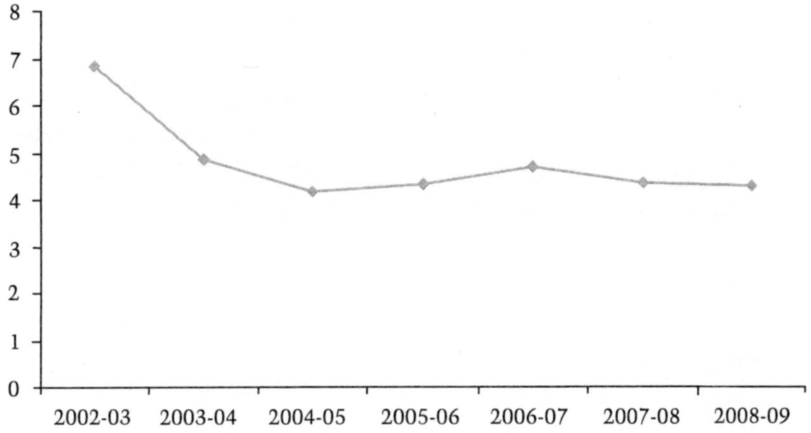

Source: Compiled from Annual Reports.

Measures to Reduce Transmission Losses

KPTCL has embarked on a mega plan to be free from all system constraints so as to reduce T&D losses to the minimum. Unless sufficient redundancy in transmission system is provided with best infrastructure, it would be difficult to compete, as the 'open access system' is already in operation. In view of the tremendous impetus given to IT and other industries in the state, there has been a huge demand for power. The sudden spurt in demand has left the existing infrastructure inadequate to cope up with the situation. This inadequate infrastructure had resulted in overloading of transformers, lines and consequent load-shedding. KPTCL was unable to provide specified number of hours of three phase power supply to rural areas, which is essential for socioeconomic growth of the state. Out of 573 stations (66 KV, 110 KV and 220 KV) existing in the state, 392 stations are overloaded by more than 70 per cent of the capacity, which as per grid code should be maintained below 70 per cent. More than 64 stations were loaded at more than 100 per cent of capacity. Similarly, there were large number of overloaded lines, which needed to be uprated or upgraded. Voltage problems were being faced in many pockets of the state. In view of deficiency in infrastructure over the years, a huge gap had been created between the target and achievements. The perspective plan for the 10th and 11th Plan showed a backlog of over 300 stations at the end of the 10th Plan. In order to combat all these problems, it was very much essential to take up all the backlog works to ensure proper power supply to the consumers. This also included augmentation of 189 stations and providing about 95 number of transmission link lines. This was to ensure some cushion, to take care of contingency conditions. Another point of contention was the load growth. The load growth is on the very high side, particularly, in Bangalore city. It ranges from 4.67 per cent to 14 per cent in Bangalore city. The high load growth is due to the growth of IT/BT and other connected industries. Additionally, Karnataka Electricity Regulatory Commission (KERC) desired KPTCL not to discriminate between urban and rural areas. All this meant substantial investment to improve infrastructure. To bring down the T&D losses in the state on par with international standards, a systematic time-bound action plan will be made to reduce both technical and commercial losses in the system.

Supervisory Control and Data Acquisition (SCADA): To reduce the outage time and also manual intervention, total SCADA of all stations in KPTCL and ESCOMs has been taken up and is to be completed by the end of 2008. This also envisages real time data regarding load, line profile for congestion, etc., so as to monitor power system. The approximate cost of the scheme is ₹ 200 crore.

IT intervention is being focused in the following areas:

- Load forecasting.
- System studies.
- Network planning and construction.

- IT enabled energy accounting.
- Loss assessment and energy audit.
- Geographic information system (GIS) mapping.
- Outages planning.
- Congestion management.
- Monitoring quality transmission.
- IT enabled station log books.
- Documents management.
- Real time management of ABT through SCADA.

The present level of transmission losses is around 4.7 per cent, which is almost in a comparable range with international standards. However, KPTCL plans to reduce the losses equal to or below 4 per cent during the 11th Plan period. KPTCL has established 72 sub-stations of various voltage levels, adding a total capacity of 1278.70 MVA during 2008-09. Two 220 KV stations, namely Nittur and Bangalore International Airport Limited (BAIL), have been commissioned. The capacity of 101 sub-stations has been enhanced by higher capacity adding 1622.20 MVA. The power transmission system strengthening was done by adding 811.36 ckms new transmission lines of different voltage levels for reducing the transmission loss. The transmission loss has been provisionally worked out at 4.7 per cent. Total outlay of ₹ 2,700 crore for the years 2006-07 for annual programme of capital works of KPTCL was approved. 346 numbers of new proposals/strengthening works detailed project reports were prepared. During 2008-09, 11 technical advisory committee meetings were conducted, which cleared 134 new sub-stations to be added in the transmission grid. For strengthening of transmission line and augmenting the stations capacity, 8 technical coordination meetings was conducted, clearing 254 works. During 2008-09, 6 independent power producer (IPP) meetings were held for evacuating 63 IPPs power generation. During 2008-09, 214 new works were under execution and 81 new works were tendered.

KPTCL has supplied energy to various units like BESCOM, MESCOM, HESCOM, GESCOM, CESC and HUKKERI. The highest energy supplied was to BESCOM.

Figure 3.2

Energy Supplied by KPTCL

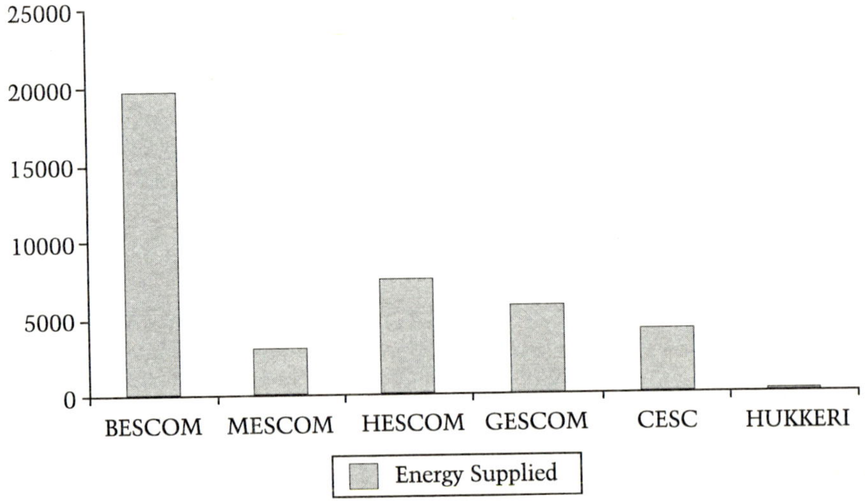

Source: Compiled from Annual Reports.

Sources of Revenue

KPTCL gets revenue from various sources by selling the power. The highest revenue comes from Bangalore Electricity Supply Corporation Limited, MESCOM, CESE, HESCOM, GESCOM (Figure 3.3).

Figure 3.3

Sources of Revenue

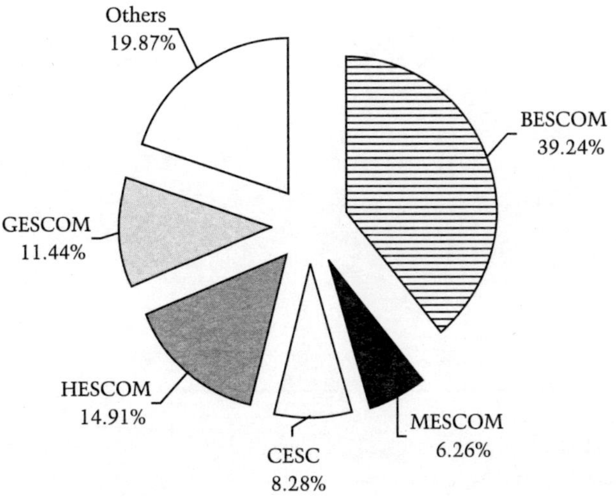

Source: Compiled from Annual Reports.

The company spends on various issues like:

Figure 3.4

Company's Expenditure on Various Issues

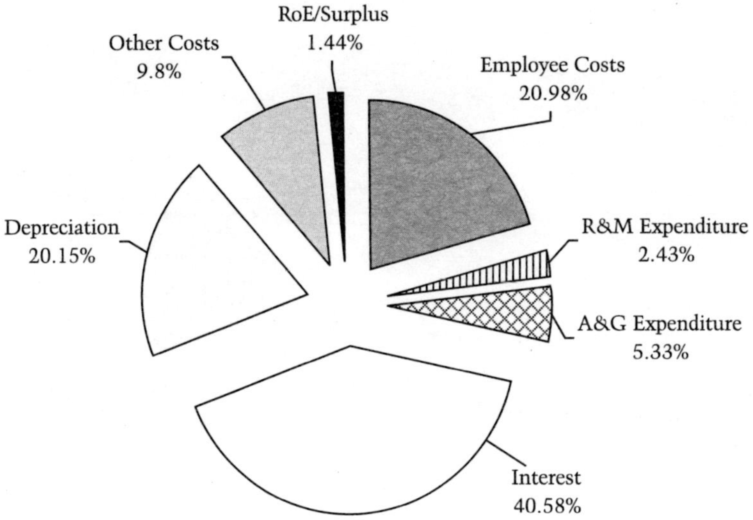

Source: Compiled from Annual Reports.

Table 3.1

Targets and Achievements during the Financial Year 2008-09

No.	Tr. Zone	Station		Line		Augmentation		Expenditure Crore
		Target	Achievement	Target	Achievement	Target	Achievement	
1.	Banglore	25	21	25	24	15	14	499.25
2.	Tumkur	16	19	16	23	8	2	225.28
3.	Mysore	16	14	16	16	5	4	134.95
4.	Hassan	15	14	15	19	10	2	229.08
5.	Bagalkote	15	17	15	25	7	17	347.77
6.	Gulbarga	13	16	13	17	5	4	198.67
7.	Admin. Offices							182.30
	Total	100	101	100	124	50	43	1817.39

Note: 1. 2,06,320.53 km HT line has been drawn.
2. The total installed capacity is 9246 MW.
3. 4,55,099.8 km LT line has been drawn.
4. 7,254 additional distribution transformer centres have been established.
5. 212 ckms transmission line was extended during the year 2009-10.

Source: Compiled from Annual Reports.

Table 3.2

KPTCL at a Glance

	2008-09	*2009-10*
Installed Capacity	9249	9249
No. of Consumers	1.66	1.67
No. of stations	1217	1232
HT Lines	204661.2	206320.5
LT Lines	453687.5	455099.8

Source: Compiled from Annual Reports.

Fixed assets of a business are the facilities needed to earn its revenues. The fixed asset turnover ratio computes how many times the outlay on these facilities have been covered by the revenues earned. The higher the turnover, the better the performance, indicating effective utilisation of the assets, and also avoiding unnecessary investment in facilities. Looking at another way, fixed assets turnover ratio measures how well the company's investment decisions turned out.

Table 3.3

Fixed Assets/Sales

Years	*Fixed Assets*	*Sales*	*Ratio*
2003-04	2070.82	6565.99	3.17
2004-05	2262.86	6774.92	2.99
2005-06	2377.65	2155.24	0.91
2006-07	2705.10	966.9	0.36
2007-08	3675.12	969	0.26
2008-09	4907.16	972.55	0.20

Source: Compiled from Annual Reports.

For one rupee of investment, the sales are at 3.17. There is a decrease in sales to investment.

Figure 3.5

Fixed Assets/Sales

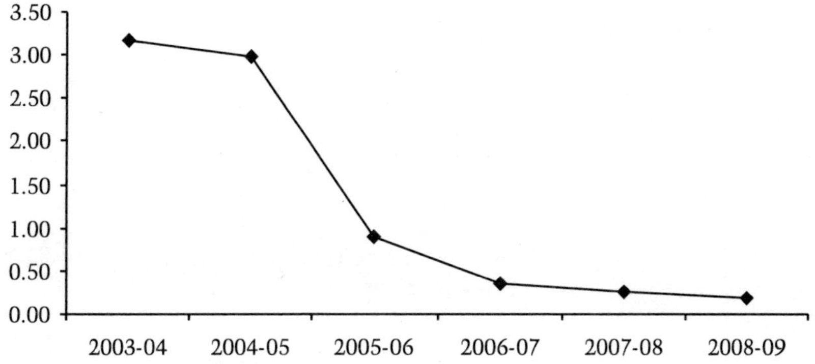

Source: Compiled from Annual Reports.

Evaluation of Financial Performance of KPTCL

Capital Structure

At the close of March 31, 2009, the paid-up capital of the corporation stood at ₹ 1,033.00 crore. Out of the total capital, the state government has the major share. The capital structure of the company for the last 6 years is shown in Figure 3.6.

Figure 3.6

Capital Structure: Equity

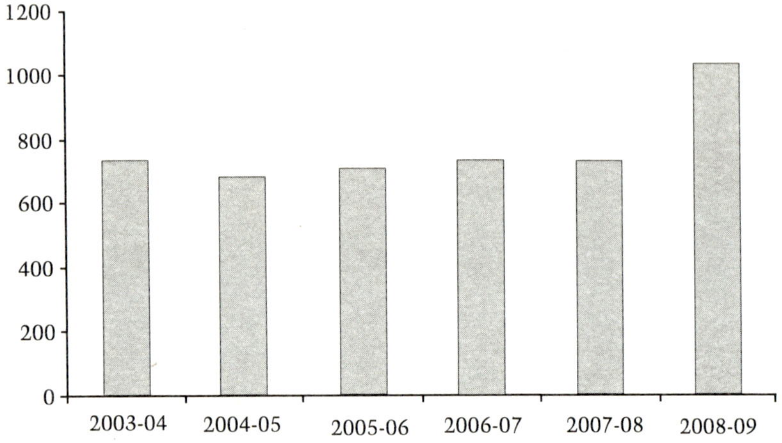

Source: Compiled from Annual Reports.

Reserves and Surplus

The reserves and surplus accumulated till March 31, 2009, was ₹ 308.88 crore as against ₹ 280.7 crore as on March 31, 2008. The reserves and surplus of the company for the last 6 years are shown in Figure 3.7.

Figure 3.7

Reserves and Surplus

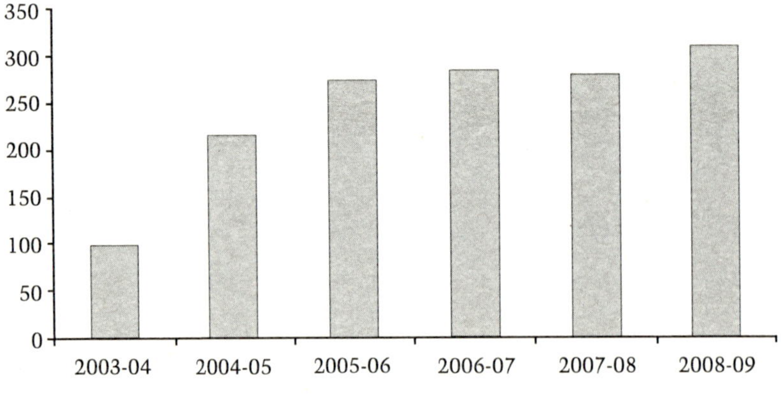

Source: Compiled from Annual Reports.

Profit Before Interest and Taxes

The company profit has not showed a remarkable progress over the years 2003-04 to 2008-09. This is mainly due to the pricing activity of the power. The power price per kilowatt is very less during 2008-09, i.e., 19.42. Added to this, the company is planning to reduce the transmission losses. This is clearly explained in Figure 3.8.

Figure 3.8

Profit Before Interest and Taxes

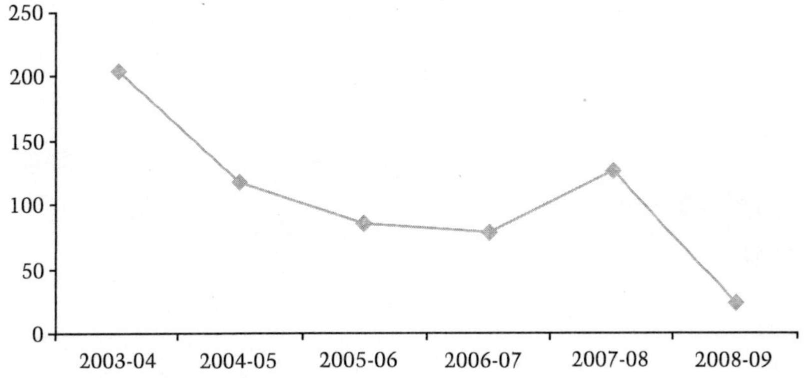

Source: Compiled from Annual Reports.

Liquidity Ratios

Liquidity ratios measures the corporation's ability to meet current obligations. The two ratios *viz.*, current ratio and quick ratio are analysed here. The current ratio is a measure of the corporate short-term solvency. It indicates the availability of current assets in rupees for every one rupee of current liability. A ratio greater than one means that the corporation has more current assets than current liabilities. During the years 2003-04 and 2005-06, the current ratio was good, but in the recent years, the company is having more current liabilities than current assets. If the situation continues, the company will fall into a liability trap. This is clearly explained in Table 3.4 and Figure 3.9.

Table 3.4

Current Ratio

Years	*Current Assets*	*Current Liabilities*	*Current Ratio*
2003-04	6264.52	4323.01	1.45
2004-05	6154.64	4254.25	1.45
2005-06	5454.31	4037.00	1.35
2006-07	4039.18	4196.85	0.96
2007-08	4448.03	5093.04	0.87
2008-09	4233.23	4617.94	0.92

Source: Compiled from Annual Reports.

Figure 3.9

Current Ratio

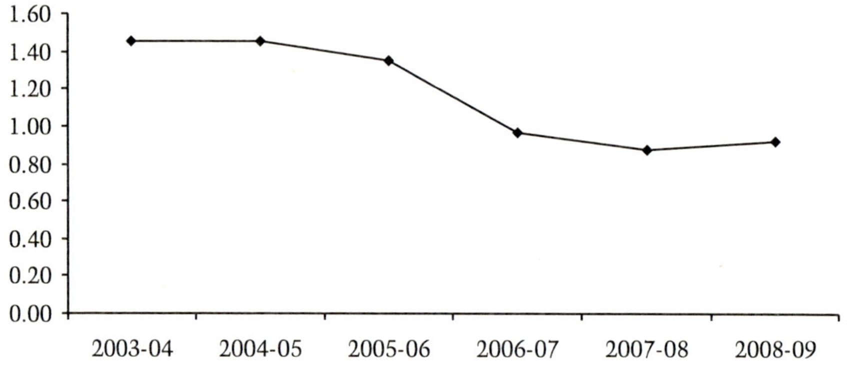

Source: Compiled from Annual Reports.

Leverage Ratios

Leverage ratios show the proportions of debt and equity in financing the firm's assets. It is clear from Table 3.5 that the lenders contribution is less than one rupee, if the owners contribution is one rupee. It is only during the years 2004-05 to 2006-07 that the lenders contribution is more than one rupee of owner's contribution. Debt equity ratio is directly computed by dividing total debt by net worth. The debt equity ratio of the company was moved from 5.08:1 in 2003-04 to 2.18:1 in 2007-08.

Table 3.5

Debt/Equity Ratio

Years	*Debt/Equity*
2003-04	5.08
2004-05	5.36
2005-06	4.54
2006-07	3.23
2007-08	2.18

Source: Compiled from Annual Reports.

Figure 3.10

Debt-Equity Ratio

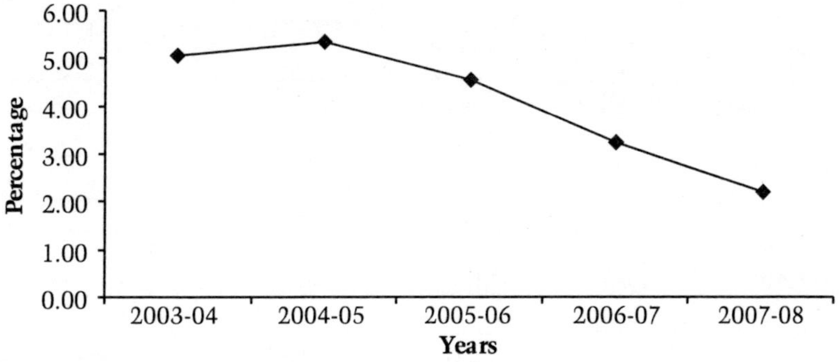

Source: Compiled from Annual Reports.

Return on Sales (ROS) Ratio

This ratio is widely used to evaluate an enterprises operational efficiency. ROS is also known as a firm's 'operating profit margin.' It is calculated using the formula, 'Profit Before Depreciation Interest and Taxes/ Sales.' This measure is helpful to management and provides an insight into how much profit is being produced per rupee of sales. As with many ratios, it is best to compare the enterprise's ROS over time to look for trends, and also compare it with similar PEs. An increasing ROS indicates that the enterprise is growing more efficiently, while a decreasing ROS could signal looming financial troubles. The company experiences a good ROS till

Figure 3.11

Return on Sales (ROS) Ratio

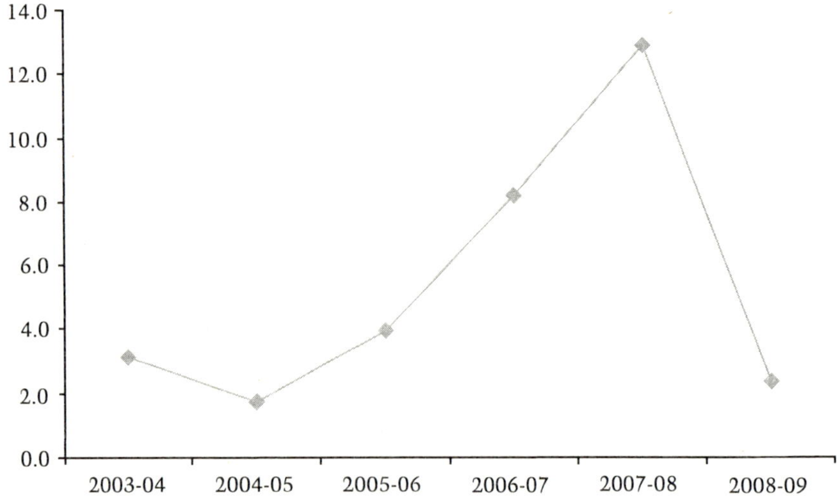

Source: Compiled from Annual Reports.

2007-08, but in recent years due to the fluctuations in power tariff, the company has experienced a decrease in ROS.

Return on Assets (ROA) Ratio

ROA is an indicator of how profitable an enterprise is relative to its total assets. ROA gives an idea as to how efficient management is at using its assets to generate earnings. Calculated by dividing an enterprise's annual earnings by its total assets, ROA is displayed as a percentage. Sometimes this is referred to as 'return on investment.' ROA explains the earnings that were generated from invested capital (assets). ROA for public companies can vary substantially and will be highly dependent on the industry. This is why when using ROA as a comparative measure, it is best to compare it against the enterprise's previous ROA numbers or the ROA of a similar enterprise. The assets of the enterprise comprises both debt and equity. Both of these types of financing are used to fund the operations of

Figure 3.12

Return on Assets (ROA) Ratio

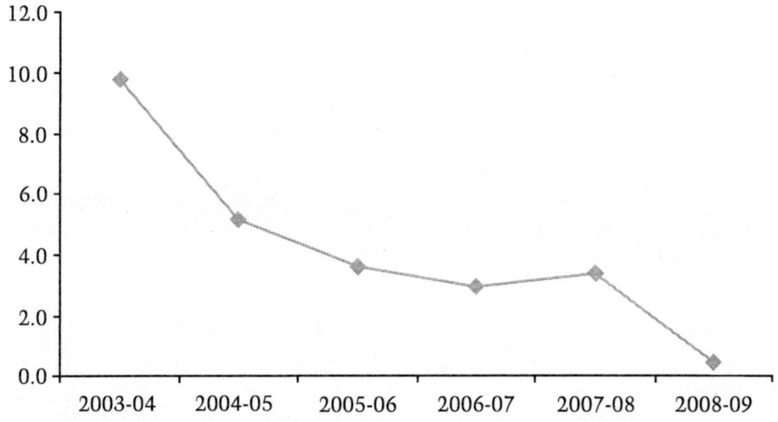

Source: Compiled from Annual Reports.

the enterprise. The ROA figure gives investors an idea of how effectively the enterprise is converting the money it has to invest into net income. The higher the ROA number the better, because the enterprise is earning more money on less investment. This ROA has experienced a drastic fall during 2007-08 and 2008-09.

Return on Equity (ROE) Ratio

ROE is a measure of the profitability that reveals how much profit the enterprise is generating with the money that shareholders have invested. ROE is useful for comparing the profitability of an enterprise with that of other firms in the same industry. Figure 3.13 shows that the ROE is at its highest during the years 2007-08 and it has experienced a steady decline in progress over the years.

Figure 3.13

Return On Equity

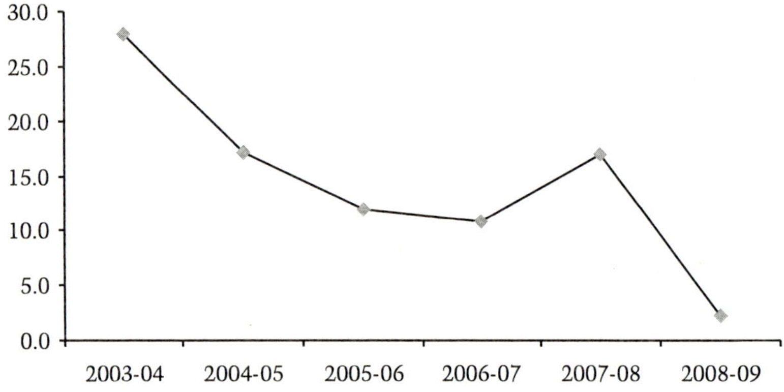

Source: Compiled from Annual Reports.

Table 3.6

Profitability Ratios

	ROS	*ROA*	*ROE*
2003-04	3.1	9.9	27.9
2004-05	1.7	5.2	17.2
2005-06	4.0	3.6	12.0
2006-07	8.2	2.9	10.8
2007-08	12.9	3.4	17.0
2008-09	2.3	0.5	2.2

Source: Compiled from Annual Reports.

Table 3.7

Strengths, Weaknesses, Opportunities and Threats (SWOT) Analysis

Strengths	*Opportunities*
• Monopoly in business. • The company has huge network for transmission of power. • Good infrastructure facilities. • The company has got better human resource for carrying on the operations effectively.	• KPTCL proposes further lines for enriching the power supply to new segment areas, thereby, the availability of power will be enhanced. • The company will make use of new technology transmission lines by keeping in view AAAC (all aluminium alloy conductors). • Because of the above, the performance of the company will further improve and transmission losses will come down. • It is also suggested that controlling points for the leakages can be arrested by using higher technology and also adopting the key measures.
Weakness	*Threats*
• The major weakness of the company is that the pricing policy is not in the hands of the company. • The company has to further strengthen the human resource with enrichment of skills. • The transmission losses work out to 4.7 per cent on average when compared to global transmission standards i.e., around 3.5 per cent. • Poor maintenance of transmission systems.	• The response of the public is negative. • Collection of bills is not appropriate inorder to meet the costs of the company. • The illegal power connections are effecting the performance of the company, and hence, the company has to take certain measures for accounting the power so that the utilisation factor will go up.

Summary and Recommendations

- Inadequate attention to working capital management is the root-cause for financial embarrassments in many cases.
- Quick rotation of the current assets brings down the working capital needs, which is considered as a hallmark of any successful business organisation.

- Greater focus on result oriented/pragmatism/commercial orientation.
- Greater focus on adoptability/flexibility/responsiveness to market changes.
- Greater delegation of powers/empowering.
- Division of responsibility at higher levels.
- Greater use of matrix structure of management.
- Creation of new roles within functions.
- Delayering/reduction in the number of layers.
- Improvement of skills by training/counselling/job rotation, etc.
- Other empowering actions at workshop level.

4 Karnataka State Police Housing Corporation Ltd

J. Kiranmai

Introduction

Karnataka State Police Housing Corporation Ltd (KSPHC) was established in 1985, as a special purpose vehicle (SPV), to cater to the housing requirements—both residential and non-residential—of the police and the allied departments. KSPHC's vision is to adopt best practices, pursue emerging opportunities and to become an attractive market leader for both avenues i.e., for investors as well as a service provider to the public. During 2006-07, the corporation has executed works worth ₹ 87.65 crore, with a total number of 812 residential buildings and 78 non-residential buildings. The corporation has divisional offices at Bengaluru (2), Mysore, Shimoga, Davanagere, Belgaum and Gulbarga, and subdivisions at Bengaluru (3), Kolar, Mysore, Hassan, Chamarajanagar, Shimoga, Mangalore, Chickmaglur, Belgaum, Bagalkote, Dharwad, Gulbarga, Raichur, Bijapur, Davangere, Haveri and Koppal. The organisation has been classified under development enterprises in non-commercial category by the Department of Disinvestment and Public Enterprises Reforms, Government of Karnataka (GoK). The corporation forms a part of the Home and Transport Department,[1] GoK. Among the Home and Transport Department, there are five transportation corporation and KSPHC is the only one non-commercial development corporation. During 2004, a Police Science Congress, DSGP/ISPG Conference was held in Gujarat, where the need for ISO certification in police departments was emphasised. They also quoted that in this regard the two enterprises i.e., Delhi Police and Police Housing Corporation of Karnataka have obtained these certifications. This

1. *Performance Report of the State Public Enterprises, 2005-06*, DPE, GoK.

would help the police department to document all their activities, and would make the system more efficient and would also help constantly to improve quality.

Objectives of KSPHC

The main objectives to be pursued by the KSPHC as per its Memorandum of Association are the following:

- To undertake construction of buildings for housing the employees of the GoK in the police, prisons, home guards and fire force department.
- To undertake construction of buildings for the offices of the departments of police, prisons, home guards such as the administrative offices, police stations, jails, fire stations, training institutions, district scientific laboratories, forensic science laboratories, dormitaries, etc.
- To construct schools, hospitals, health centres, shops, clubs, auditoriums, maternity homes, *kalyana mantaps*, etc., that will be built out of the police benevolent fund and also to undertake construction of any type of buildings entrusted to it by the government from time to time.

Vision and Mission

KSPHC vision and mission is discussed as follows.

Vision Statement

"To organise ourselves as total quality people to achieve world class standards in all our endeavours and be role model for excellence in public service."

Mission Statement

- To improve competency and to meet the changing needs of business for e-Governance.
- To achieve sustainable development through quality construction service.

- To maintain quality standards by adopting quality management systems.

Activities

The primary activity of KSPHC is to construct buildings, both residential and non-residential for the police, fire force, prison and other government departmensts. The corporation has constructed and handed over 17,198 residential and 751 non-residential buildings, since inception.

Management

KSPHC is fully owned by the GoK. As on March 31, 2007, the paid-up capital of KSPHC is ₹ 12 lakh. Loan received during the year is ₹ 28 crore. The total investment of the enterprise is ₹ 28.86 crore and the GoK holds 0.73 per cent of the total investment. Hundred per cent of the shares are held by the GoK. The composition of Board of Directors of KSPHC is depicted in Table 4.1.

Table 4.1

Board of Directors

Name	*Designation*
S.C. Saxena, IPS	Chairman and Managing Director, KSPHC
Prem Shankar Meena, IAS	Executive Director
T. Suneel Kumar	Home Secretary, GoK
Jija Madhavan Hari Singh, IPS	DGP & Commandant General Home Guards, and Director Civil Defence and Fire & Emergency Services, GoK
D.V. Guruprasad, IPS	ADGP Recruitment & Training, Bangalore
M.R Kamble, IPS	Secretary, Finance Department (PMR), GoK
T. Sukumar	Secretary PWD, GoK
M.K. Srivatsava, IPS	ADGP, TTM

Source: Compiled from Annual Reports.

Manpower

KSPHC has a sanctioned strength of 321 personnel in various cadres. There are 79 permanent employees, 83 are on deputation and 73 are temporary employees. Apart from the temporary employees, the organisation also provides employment to casual labour in their construction sites.

Financial Performance

The corporation is working on 'no profit–no loss.' Therefore, the adjustments of the revenue accounts are made by transferring the excess expenditure over the revenue to works-in-progress account. Therefore, the usual financial norms and management ratios are not applicable in this case. Nevertheless the activities of the corporation can be understood based on the turnover. The corporation has received ₹ 10.55 crore as deposit from the police department under Eleventh Finance Commission. As a part of the fund, KSPHC has constructed 130 rest rooms and toilets for women police employees and also 54 police stations. Table 4.2 presents the financial position, which includes the total equity, total debt, investment, networth, capital employed, revenues earned, gross margin and profit before interest and tax of KSPHC during 2000-01 to 2006-07.

Table 4.2

Financial Position of KSPHC

(in crore)

Financial Year	*State Equity*	*Other Equity*	*Total Equity*	*State Debt*	*Other Debt*	*Total Debt*	*Total Investment*	*Net Worth*	*Capital Employed*
2000-01	0.12	0	0.12	0	70.09	70.09	70.21	0.12	70.21
2001-02	0.12	0	0.12	0	132.54	132.54	132.66	0.12	132.66
2002-03	0.12	0	0.12	0	0	0	0	0.12	0
2003-04	0.12	0	0.12	0				0.12	247.62
2004-05	0.12	0	0.12	0	255.00	255.00	355.69	0.12	255.00
2005-06	0.12	0	0.12	0	288.50	288.50	288.62	0.12	288.50
2006-07	0.12	0	0.12	0	280.92	280.92	281.04	0.12	280.92

Source: Institute of Public Enterprise (IPE) Database on SLPEs.

The corporation is raising loans from financial institutions. The outstanding loan during 2006-07 was ₹ 280.91 crore and the weighted average rate of interest was 9.05 per cent, whereas during 2004-05, the loan amount was ₹ 255.56 crore with a weighted average rate of interest 8.45 per cent.

Cost of Construction

Table 4.3 depicts the cost of construction of the corporation, since 2001-02 to 2006-07.

Table 4.3

Cost of Construction

(₹ in crore)

Particulars	*2006-07*	*2005-06*	*2004-05*	*2003-04*	*2002-03*	*2001-02*
Cost of Buildings completed and handed over	10605	6420	6342	13641	8337	3145
Cost of Work in progress	509.79	463.16	377.88	303.51	225.67	138.73
Borrowings	23.00	55.00	30.03	73.77	78.27	73.68
Direct Work Expenditure	65.11	102.01	88.35	81.95	86.77	100.80
Personnel Expenditure	4.49	4.26	4.03	4.12	3.24	1.78
Administrative Expenditure	2.10	1.75	2.19	1.31	1.09	0.56
Other Income	2.02	0.94	0.88	1.08	0.56	0.46
Interest Income	6.84	1.17	1.25	1.34	2.80	0.86

Source: Compiled from Annual Reports.

The income generated by the corporation from associated activities includes other income and interest income. It is seen that the generation of income is increasing, which shows that the corporation is becoming self-reliant and is seeking new avenues to meet its establishment and administrative costs.

Physical Performance

Table 4.4 depicts the status of buildings handed over/under construction, since inception till date. The corporation has handed over 18,009 residential and 830 non-residential buildings, since inception. During 2006-07, 1,819 residential buildings and 184 non-residential buildings are under construction.

Table 4.4

Status of Buildings Handed Over/Under Construction

	No. of Buildings Handed Over			*No. of Buildings Under Construction*		
	Residential	*Non-residential*	*Total*	*Residential*	*Non-residential*	*Total*
2007-08	812	78	890	1861	184	2045
2006-07	2612	83	2695	2160	154	2314
2005-06	1268	148	1416	4546	160	4706
2004-05	634	214	848	5461	192	5653
2003-04	2765	261	3026	1036	296	1332
2002-03	2739	5	2744	3283	423	3706
2001-02	1274	1	1275	4937	3	4940
2000-01	339	3	342	851	3	854
1999-2000	64	1	65	1053	5	1058
1985-86 to 1998-99	5502	36	5538	-	-	-
Total	18009	830	18839			

Source: Compiled from Annual Reports.

All over India, KSPHC executed total works hovered around ₹ 6-7 crore a year till 2001, when police modernisation efforts got a boost with liberal assistance from both the centre and the state. KSPHC has, therefore, executed an average of ₹ 80 crore work from 2001-2007. However in the years prior to 2001 when there was no government project for execution, the company was seen to be spending as high as 150 per cent of the total project costs in a year on its administrative expenses, the company therefore became sick. During 2006-07, three major schemes were executed. They are:

- *Accelerated Housing Scheme II (AHS II)*: The scheme was sanctioned during 2002, to construct 5,000 quarters for police personnel at a cost of ₹ 160.00 crore. The share of state government was low at 25 per cent, whereas central was 75 per cent. The project was approved under police modernisation scheme. So far, 3,811 quarters have been completed and handed over and remaining are about to be completed. The physical progress achieved was 76.22 per cent, which is satisfactory. One important thing that is noted was despite escalation in the price of building material, the construction cost was kept same compared to the previous schemes.

- *Accelerated Housing Scheme–III*: Due to an increase in the police force and to meet the housing requirement of the police staff, the scheme was sanctioned by the GoK. The proposal was to construct 6,000 quarters to police personnel at a cost of ₹ 440.00 crore.
- *Non-residential Buildings*: Another major scheme for construction of non-residential buildings for the police department was sanctioned by the GoK in 2000. The scheme envisaged construction of 429 non-residential buildings in 338 locations at a cost of ₹ 124 crore.

Comparison with Other Enterprise

There are many major players both in public and private sector that are acting as competitors for KSPHC. Maharashtra Police Welfare Corporation, Kerala Police Housing and Construction Corporation, Andhra Pradesh Police Housing Corporation, Punjab Police Housing Corporation, etc., are a few state enterprises, whereas Larsen and Toubro Ltd. is the largest private sector engineering and construction company. Hindustan Constructions Company Ltd. (HCC) is another major player in public sector. The other major players in Karnataka in private sector are M/s Nagarjuna Construction, M/s Prestige Construction, M/s Shobha Developers, M/s Purvankara Constructions, etc. These entities are existing for profit and they are performing in many other diversified activities including construction, and hence, the activities of the corporations cannot be directly compared with these entities.

Reforms Initiatives

The State Legislative Committee on Administrative Reforms recommended the closure of KSPHC in 2002 on account of 'redundancy.' This threat made the management headed by Haranahalli Ramaswamy initiate transformational initiatives including enterprise project management (EPM), which helped to show astounding results. A change for the better was the slogan, which was followed to ensure that the liberal modernisation plans were prepared to the best satisfaction of all stakeholders. The following important milestones were crossed during the post-reforms period by the KSPHC:

- The organisation developed a Vision 2020 document. The document articulates KSPHC's value proposition, competitive positioning and key differentiators that will allow it to create sustainable competitive advantage. KSPHC Vision 2020 is built around three pillars: market leadership, quality and people. Vision 2020 was undertaken to guide the future course of the corporation and provide a basis for short- and mid-term business planning. KSPHC adopted a vision to become world class in all its endeavours and be a role model for excellence in public service. It set about computerising all its operations to provide total transparency and accountability. e-Tendering with reverse auction was introduced in February 2003 to award government contracts on a totally transparent mode, decided by market forces, cutting across unhealthy practices such as cartel formation, favouritism, etc. A number of initiatives were adopted as a part of the Vision 2020 that are discussed below:
    - o Web-enabled Project Management System (WBPMS): The system developed in house and deployed from January 2002, ensured colloboration and information sharing along with team building efforts to get things done successfully instead of successfully explaining why a thing could not be done. The WBPMS has become a proprietary application of KSPHC that is continually being improved upon to streamline processes and work flows in the organisation to ensure transparency and accountability while giving cost-effective and timely deliveries of goods and services to the customers—both internal and external.
    - o The Project Management System (PMS) is now being sought by other organisation for improving the delivery of their process to ensure that outcomes match outlays in government-funded projects.
    - o Quality Management System (QMS) is followed by introducing environment management system (EMS) under

ISO 14000. The computerisation in the Board was backed by following the best practices security standards i.e., BS7799. The benefits of complying with ISO 9001:2000 standards at the corporation are as follows:

(a) Reduction in process time.

(b) Less non-conformity due to systematic checks at every process.

(c) Consistency in performance.

(d) Improvement in personnel competence.

(e) Remarkable savings in overall project cost.

(f) Overall transparency in work execution.

o Metrics management system (MMS) is the tool by which KSPHC hopes to operationalise and realise its Vision 2020. MMS is many systems rolled into one. It is a performance related pay package for the employees of the corporation. It helps to measure the performance of each employee and enable a 360 degree assessment to arrive at an individual employee's contribution towards the goal of the company. An employee whose contribution is assessed to be better stands to get a better pay and reward packet compared to an employee who has underperformed or has been unable to perform due to constraints. These constraints are also taken into consideration while arriving at the overall score of performance by which his advancement and rewards, etc., are decided in the organisation. MMS is, thus, a combination of the pay rules, performance or ACR (Annual Confidential Report) rules, promotion rules, and also serves as a normalising platform for the employees serving the organisation, coming as they do from myriad organisation with diverse background and expertise in business practices and skills. MMS also attempts to cover the cadre and recruitment process as well as the disciplinary proceedings for below par performance. MMS includes a process for giving encouragement to individual capacity building and skill upgradation. In short, MMS is a unique HR tool for motivating peak performance of all employees and assisting them to climb greater heights of achievement.

- Other directives: The grants from the GoK envisaged for the years 2005 and 2006 were ₹ 79.53 crore respectively and ₹ 67.50 crore as borrowings. This plan was formulated keeping in view the requirement that all the sanctioned schemes has to be completed as per the government order. The corporation has borrowed ₹ 55.00 crore from financial institutions and GoK allocated a grants of ₹ 124.3 crore for the repayment of loan, interest and also to meet work expenditure. Despite of such allocations, the corporation could not utilise the funds, as new schemes were sanctioned by the home department, since 2003.
- The Karnataka Transparency in Public Procurement Act and the Right to Information Act were promulgated during July 2002. In June 2002, a legislative committee on Administrative Reforms recommended winding up of this company on grounds of redundancy. Amidst such tumultuous conditions, R. Sri Kumar joined as Chairman and Managing Director (CMD) in July 2001. To avert closure, a transformation initiative was formulated and Board approval was obtained on August 30, 2001, to implement a computerisation plan with the help of K.V. Prahalada Rao as an external technical consultant. The board initially authorised a budget of ₹ 4.5 million from internal accruals and later realising the potential, progressively increased the allocation to ₹ 30 million. The WBPMS went live with the launch of a portal *www.ksphc.org* on March 15, 2002, when 136 projects could be monitored from desktops, from any where. Currently, the WBPMS encompasses over 2,000 project sites. The initiative received a set back when the system integrator and hosting service provider decided to close shop in January 2003. However, this set back required that a new hosting service provider be identified, for which the corporation opted for e-Tendering and this helped usher in e-procurement. From March 2003, e-Tendering, a totally transparent mode of award of Government contracts, became a regular feature. Now after International Standards Organization

(ISO) certification in June 2005, KSPHC is offering both WBPMS and e-Tendering as paid services to other clients. For the first time since inception, KSPHC posted an excess of income over expenditure during 2006-07.

Awards and Honours

- KSPHC for its initiatives of WBPMS have earned the Golden Peacock award, the e-Governance award and the best practices award from central and state government departments, as well as from private institutions.
- Leadership in Energy and Environment Design (LEED) Rating: Cold Certification by the US Green Building Council for the Police Bhavan at Gulbarag was received.
- Government of India Award: The organisation was awarded first prize for excellence in the field of housing and human settlements.
- The GoK award, Ecology and Environment award for 2007-08: A citation and ₹ 1 lakh cash award were given on the eve of Worlds Environment Day in 2007.
- KSPHC continued to pursue a policy that promoted a strategy to change for the better. Internal processes were codified in tune with ISO. The company got its ISO 9001:2000 certification on June 10, 2005. Pleased with the perfomance of KSPHC, the State Government approved a new Memorandum of Association that now provides the organisation, the flexibility to venture into new areas of business. These include: services for infrastructure projects—to act as consulting contractors, engineers, designers and developers for infrastructure-related projects; information technology (IT) products, services and consultancy—to set up IT infrastructure to offer e-Governance and citizen services; to develop, market and operate internet portals to design, develop and market software, hardware and total IT products to act as consultants in implementing total IT solutions for industries, government establishments and R&D institutions; training—to establish, recruit for and operate a training facility for personnel who can be employed in rendering the services offered by the corporation.

KSPHC Functioning and Performance: An Analysis

This section presents an analysis of KSPHC functioning and performance. The information presented in this section is based on the information gathered from the annual reports.

SWOT Analysis

Strengths

- KSPHC has imbibed good corporate practices such as a high degree of cost consciousness, transparency in all the transactions, system changes to bring down time and cost overruns.
- The corporation has unique WBPMS through which it is monitoring the physical and financial progress of the projects. It has hailed model initiatives to evaluate other undertakings engaged in project implementation.
- The corporation is engaged in TQM practices and is working towards getting quality certification besides ISO 9001:2000.
- Offering specialised services like project management and construction of projects for central and state governments.
- Taking up maintenance work of all the police buildings, both residential and non-residential in the state.
- Mobilisation of funds through public issue of equity shares/ private placement of bonds.
- The organisation has initiated steps to introduce online process of contractors bills.

Weakness

- The corporation is engaged in executing projects assigned to it by government departments and is restricted from engaging in any other activity other than constructing buildings for these departments, which does not have any income generating activity of its own.
- The corporation is in a position to commercially exploit its resources for revenue generation.

- The corporation is supposed to run on 'no profit and no loss' basis.
- The performance of the corporation depends upon the sanctions of adequate borrowing limits in time.
- For stability and growth, the corporation needs to concentrate on human resource development. At present 60 per cent of its employees are on deputation from other departments.

Opportunities

- The corporation has undertaken online tendering process to provide transparency in the whole procurement process; there would be considerable reduction in demand on bidders cost as they need not have to travel to and from KSPHC; reduction in bidders cost, transparency, quick orders finalisation, bringing down manual errors.
- e-Billing and online payments of contractors bills.
- Introduction of e-commerce activity in 2007. Through this portal, quality building materials are supplied to the contractors at competitive rates.

Threats

- The corporation faced the threat of closure as per the recommendation of Haranahalli Ramaswamy Committee Report.
- The corporation has been entrusted with greater responsibility to implement the central government assisted police moderanisation programme. This programme helped the organisation to generate revenues.

The organisation has been able to turnaround due to the various initiatives that were undertaken during post-reforms period. It is evident that the aggregate value of work done since inception till 2001, i.e., for a period of 15 years, is less than what the organisation has achieved during 2002-2007, i.e., a period of five years. The process of transformation began in 2001 and has taken six years to achieve what was visioned. Table 4.5 indicates the path traversed by the company before, during and after the transformation.

Table 4.5

Aggregate Value of Work Done

(in crore)

Period	*Aggregate value of works (Actual/Projected)*
During 16 years from 1985 to 2001	11.84 (0.74/year)
During six years from 2001 to 2007	52.50 (875.02/year)
During five years from 2007 to 2012	10 bn (2 bn per year) (projected)

Source: Compiled from Annual Reports.

The transformation has helped KSPHC win the trust and confidence of all its customers and to become a self-reliant professionally run company working on commercial lines in a competitive environment from its earlier status of being dependent on government funds. Table 4.6 identifies the indicators of measurement of transformation. The fund allotments made from state and central governments for modernisation of police, prison and fire protection called for improved efficiency. To improve the efficiency of KSPHC and to overcome the threat of closure due to redundancy, the transformation was conceived after the CMD took charge in July 2001. With the help and recommendations of experts in the field of IT, the scheme details for the PMS were finalised. A tendering process was initiated and from amongst 30 odd competitors, the system integrator (M/s Condor Labs) and the developer (Microsoft certified partner M/s Cal-info) were selected for the implementation of the system, as these two contenders emerged as the lowest bidders. The first Beta version was tested on January 19, 2002. The project was formally commissioned in March 2002. After closure of M/s Condor Labs, M/s Bharat Sanchar Nigam Limited, a Government of India (GoI) concern, won a keenly contested e-tendering-cum-reverse auction process for the co-location contract, which was conducted by Wipro's 01 Markets Division. Microsoft published a case study of the project in February 2003 and this gave an impetus to continue with further development and enhancement in the application software. In 2005, integration of PMS with Tally accounting package was planned and the services of M/s Tally Solutions were contracted to do this job along with M/s Cal-info. The board of directors and GoK gave full support to the endeavours right through the transformation.

Table 4.6

Some Indicators of Measurement of Transformation

(in crore)

Indicators	*During 16 years prior to transformation*	*During 5 years post-transformation*
Average work done/year	74.02	875.03
Average administrative expenses/year	9.67	74.61
Average annual income	1.40	33.79
Administrative expenses as per cent of work done	3.06	8.52

Source: Compiled from Annual Reports.

Restructuring/Turnaround Management

Turnaround management may be defined as "a systematic and speedy implementation of a range of measures to correct a grave financial situation of sickness in an organisation, caused by a set of complex problems over a period of time, and to provide adequate chances for its long term survival and prosperity." As may be seen from the above, it is evident that sickness is not an unforeseen and sudden development and also it is not attributable to a single cause. Sickness is a reflection of many complex problems mounted-up over a long period. As per section 15 of Sick Industrial Companies (Special Provision) Act 1985 (SICA), a company, which is in existence for a minimum of 5 years, is considered sick only when 100 per cent or more of its net worth (capital plus free reserves) is eroded and it has also suffered cash losses (loss before providing for non-cash provisions like depreciation or deferred revenue expenditure) in such financial year, and the financial year preceding such financial year. In such cases, these companies should refer their cases to the Board for Industrial & Financial reconstruction (BIFR) for further necessary actions likc providing adequate time for revival of the company on its own within a specified period, or to suggest some revival package. The said SICA is an act, which is designed to make special provisions in the public interest, to secure the timely detection of 'sick' and 'potentially sick' companies for speedy determination and expeditious enforcement of preventive, ameliorative, remedial and other measures by an expert board. In short, this act aims to "safeguard the economy of the nation and to protect viable sick units." Similarly, the financial institutions, which provide a substantial portion of the loan funds have defined sickness in their own fashion. As per RBI, a sick company is one, 'which incurs cash loss for one year and in the judgment of the bank is likely to continue to incur losses for the current year as well as ratios such as current ratio is less than 1:1 and worsening debt equity ratio.' As per SBI, a sick unit is one 'which fails to generate internal accruals (profits) on a continuous basis and depends for its survival upon frequent infusion of funds from outside sources.' IDBI decides the sickness of a company based on some selected parameters such as consecutive defaults in the payment of institutional dues and continued cash losses.

The following are the various strategies for restructuring, which an enterprises could consider for better performance:

1. Managerial overhaul:
    - Replacement of CEO/Directors.
    - Reshuffle of senior executives.
2. Team building:
    - Greater cohesion and emphasis on survival.
    - New top management committees.
    - New/enhanced formal participative/democratic management structures.
    - Consensus decision-making in groups.
    - Stronger HRD teams, conflict resolution programmes.
3. Stress on discipline:
    - Greater focus on discipline.
    - Greater focus on punctuality at all levels.
    - Greater focus on accountability.
    - Greater focus on professionalism.
    - Greater focus on participation/empowerment/teamwork.
    - Greater focus on caring culture.
    - Greater focus on technocratic culture.

4. Strategic shift:
    - Mergers/acquisitions/joint ventures/partnerships.
    - Shift towards core competencies.
    - Shift towards high growth segments/markets.
    - Vender development.
    - Shift towards high-tech products.
    - Shift towards faster product development/differentiation.
    - Stronger price leadership/market dominance.
    - Lower cost/price strategies.
    - Other competitive initiatives.
5. Capital restructuring:
    - Induction of fresh equity.
    - Induction of long term loans.
    - Reduction of long term debts.
    - Liquidation of other current assets.
    - Reduction in short term barrowings.
6. Asset and cost surgery:
    - Divestiture of capital assets including plants/divisions/ facilities.
    - Closure of uneconomic plants/facilities.
7. Financial mending:
    - Tighter controls over cash disbursements.
    - Tighter controls over purchases.
    - Tighter controls over capital expenditure.
    - Tighter controls over credit facilities to customers.
    - Tighter controls over inventory.
    - Quick liquidation of stocks.

- Quick liquidation of debtors.
- Cut in employee related benefits/wage freezes/deferment of promotions.
- Voluntary retirement of employees/layoffs.
- Planned reduction in sales and distribution, and administration expenses.
- Reduction in rent.
- Energy saving.
- Extensive use of outsourcing, if found economical.
- Reduction in R&D expenditure.

8. Manpower restructuring:
    - Redeployment after training for higher skills/improved productivity.
    - Reduction of manpower/retrenchment.
    - Golden shake hand/ voluntary retirement.
9. Productivity and quality:
    - Greater focus on quality/efficiency/productivity/economy.
    - Greater focus on innovativeness/entrepreneurship.
    - Greater focus on result oriented/pragmatism/commercial orientation.
    - Greater focus on adoptability/flexibility/responsiveness to market changes.
    - Greater focus on efficiency/productivity/economy.
    - Greater focus on innovativeness/entrepreneurship.
    - Greater focus on result-oriented/pragmatism/commercial orientation.
    - Greater focus on adoptability/flexibility/responsiveness to market changes.

10. Organisational restructuring:
    - Setting up of new groups/strategic business units (SBUs)/ divisions/profit centres, etc.
    - Greater delegation of powers/empowering.
    - Division of responsibility at higher levels.
    - Greater use of matrix structure of management.
    - Creation of new roles within functions.
    - Delayering/reduction in the number of layers.
    - Improvement of skills by training/counseling/job rotation, etc.
    - Other empowering actions at workshop level.
11. Sales/revenue focus:
    - New advertisements and sales promotion campaigns.
    - Price cuts/incentives to customers.
    - Increased/improved distribution channels.
    - Entry in to new domestic.
    - Export push.
    - Better services to customers.
    - Better plant repairs and maintenance.
    - Standardisation.
    - Automation/computerisation of operations.
    - Induction of more capable supervisors.
    - New systems and procedures.
    - Better production/operation norms.
    - Bench marking.
    - Introduction of new systems of production scheduling/ planning and other industrial engineering activities.

12. Management communications:

    - Mass communication using news letters, audio-visual means, internet, slogans, etc., explaining the causes and the suggested remedial actions.
    - Involving staff in turnaround exercises to assess the gravity of the situation, and for suggested remedial actions right from the lowest rungs.
    - Face to face meetings of the top level with the lowest workmen (*mukha-mukhi*).
    - Public recognitions/awards for excellent contributions.

Summary of Findings and Suggestions

- The findings of the study offers some suggestions to make the SLPEs financially viable. KSPHC has envisioned becoming the first government organisation to establish an integrated management system, encompassing the following management system standards:
    - o Quality Management System.
    - o Environment Management System.
    - o Occupational Health System.
    - o Social Accountability System.
    - o IT System.
    - o Quality Management System.
- The enterprise owes their existence more to the historical factors and pragmatism than ideological considerations. The enterprise came into existence on account of the historical necessity. The enterprise have to undertake promotional activities and provide infrastructure support.
- The organisation has been categorised under development enterprises (non-commercial). The categorisation of the enterprise can be rescheduled so that the commercialisation of its operations would be given more emphasis.

- The enterprise typology points out that the relative importance of different kinds of enterprises that were prioritised by the state in view of their socioeconomic strategy.
- The high debt-equity ratio posed a great financial threat to the SLPEs.
- The financial performance of the enterprises was satisfactory during the study period.
- The restructuring modalities differ from situation to situation. However, some commonly used approaches which may be resorted for restructuring include public flotation, private placement, trade sale, management buyouts and transfer to workers' cooperatives.
- The enterprise diversified its activities during the post-reforms period. This diversification used on information technology to improve performance efficiency.
- The state governments in general, prefer to run only such SLPEs that have an important social purpose to serve and that are financially viable.

Suggestions

We offer the following strategic suggestions for the restructuring and performance improvement of the SLPEs.

- Such of the SLPEs, which cannot keep their net worth intact, may be wound up. Their activities may be handed over to the concerned administrative departments of the state governments. The central philosophy behind setting up SLPEs to undertake such activities was that they should be transacting them on the commercial basis.
- KSPHC was recommended the closure during 2002, on account of redundancy, the organisation has recovered with a speedy determination. Change for better was the motto and helped the organisation to become healthy. The organisation has been categorised under development enterprises (non-commercial). The categorisation of the enterprise can be rescheduled, so that the commercialisation of operations would be given more emphasis.

KSPHC needs to focus on the important initatives, which include human resource aspects, technological aspects, financial aspects and organisational aspects.

- The state governments could follow the three-dimensional matrix approach (i.e., relating the SLPEs to parameters such as social purpose, resource mobilisation and profitability) to identify their portfolio of the SLPEs for retentions. The enterprises that are 'Low' on all the three scores could be divested, whereas the enterprises being 'High' on all these three score could be retained. The enterprises falling in between these two categories should be dealt differently.
- Aggressive recruitment of human resources both through internal channels of deputation and market-oriented recruitment was adapted by the corporation.
- The organisation need to strengthen the manpower requirement.
- Increasing the capacity/capability building to ensure that KSPHC personnels emerge as subject matter experts/consultants and can assist clients (both in the public and private sector).
- Provision for additional capital: transformational restructuring programme entails to a provision of additional capital. This may be required for modernaisation and repair of plant and machinery. The additional capital has to be provided on concessional terms, at least for the initial years, so that the financial burden on the unit is not high.
- Internal audit (IA) system should be developed. The IA is often involved in the preparation and review of financial statements. It also attends to activities pertaining to the control of frauds. These precisely include fraud detection and fraud investigation. The IA is not consulted in the design and development stage of new or revised programmes and systems.
- Memorandum of Understanding (MoU) system should be developed. The MoU system should be a part of the long-term performance evaluation exercise covering a period of five years.

Such an arrangement would give a reasonable time for the fair trial of the MoU as an innovative concept.

- Corporate plan has to be designed keeping in view the vision document. The corporate plan can be prepared for a longer period.
- Modernisation of technology to compete with other market players.

The study observed that the overall performance of the KSPHC has improved both financially and physically, since 2001. The Vision Document created a path for transformation of KSPHC to adopt best practices for better performance improvement.

The state enterprise being the second largest component of the public enterprise system in India has to initiate reforms and restructuring to meet the challenges of financial viability posed by economic reforms.

5 Bangalore Metropolitan Transport Corporation Limited

S.K. Mathur

Introduction

In Karnataka, passenger road transport was being catered to by a single corporation called the Karnataka State Road Transport Corporation (KSRTC). However, it was felt by Government of Karnataka (GoK) that a single monolith enterprise would be having the inherent disadvantage of centralisation and consequent slower decision-making and such a structure would not meet the needs of the corporation, which operates in a dynamic environment and deals with meeting the demand of passenger traffic, which has to be met at the time of the day or period when it arises, lest it shift to other means of transport such as rail. or to private buses. Hence, as per the recommendation of the committee on restructuring, KSRTC was spilt into four distinct entities, namely:

- Karnataka State Road Transport Corporation (KSRTC).
- Bangalore Metropolitan Transport Corporation (BMTC).
- North Western Karnataka Road Transport Corporation (NWKRTC).
- North Eastern Karnataka Road Transport Corporation (NEKRTC).

The reorganisation through the splitting process was commenced in 1997 and completed in steps by October 2000, through creation of the aforesaid four independent corporations. The first to be created as a consequence of the restructuring of the composite KSRTC was the Bangalore Metropolitan Transport Corporation (BMTC) in 1997.

Methodology for the Analysis of Performance of BMTC

KSRTC has indeed shown dynamism from the time the corporation split has been initiated. as is evidenced from the performance statistics. For the purpose of this study, its performance has been analysed for management of the enterprise for the following points of view.

- Resource utilisation: Examining the utilisation of the various assets, namely machines (buses), men, materials, money; and other assets, namely, lands and buildings.
- Decision-making: Identifying areas needing yet further improvement and need for an improvised MIS.
- Stakeholders concerns: Government, society, commuters, employees & management. especially with respect to quality and safety of the transport service provided
- Strategy management: Adoption of strategy to match the changing economic and technological environment for competitive advantage, especially in view of seasonality of passenger traffic demands.

The management of a complex and dynamic business such as passenger road transport has been viewed in the context of the upheavals on the international economic front, mainly:

- Hitherto existing uptrend in petroleum and oil prices witnessed in the first half of the financial year 2008-09, and
- The recent global financial meltdown, which has led to capital erosion, liquidity crunch and slump in consumption across various sectors including downslide in consumption of services such as transportation by air rail/road at least for purposes of leisure travel, comprising trips for shopping and entertainment in urban areas.

The aforesaid two events have indeed taught all business enterprises a hither lesson of anticipating such crises and getting prepared with strategies to combat them, so that, in future, the organisation is better prepared for such a hostile environment, which adversely impacts the performance of the organisations. Yet, another dimension of the study is to examine the prospect of collaborative strategy for business, as well as scope for growth through radically different models such as the franchise model at least in some areas.

Outsourcing of some activities, multi-skilling of staff, automation/ adoption of relevant information technology, etc.

SWOT Analysis of BMTC

Strengths

- BMTC has a good infrastructure comprising depots with good fleet maintenance facilities, bus stations at many cities, towns, in various districts and *talukas*, a widespread IT infrastructure with networks spanning across all its depots, divisions, workshops and stores, etc.
- Its bus fleet is quite young at about 3.4 lakh kilometers and this gives the corporation, the advantage of lesser propensity for breakdowns of buses in operation and hence, lesser cancellation of bus services and thereby, the commuters would patronise its bus services in preference to costlier modes such as autorickshaws.
- Progressive top management team, which adopts innovative practices and adopts state-of-the art IT to improve efficiency and to reduce costs.
- Downsized workforce, making BMTC cost-competitive in providing passenger services.
- Land at depots and bus stations, which lend substantial potential for developing revenue yielding projects such as commercial complexes, shopping malls, etc.
- A large number of bus depots, with at least 2 or 3 depots in the vicinity which can act as stand-by depots in case of one of these depots remaining inoperative due to natural calamities, strikes, etc.

Weaknesses

- A large number of clandestinely operating private buses which make inroad into their revenues and compete with BMTC's services.

- There is a need to go in for borrowing to fund the various programmes such as fleet augmentation with number of Volvo, AC, deluxe, luxury and ordinary coaches, as well as for capital-intensive bus station projects, IT projects, etc.
- The delay in receipt of subsidies from government such as concessional bus passes etc., were not regularly supported by the government.
- The obligation of operating at least few trips in a day to connect small, remote villages even at low occupancy ratio causing losses, being a state level organisation more as a welfare measure.
- Less satisfactory safety track record in the country: They are recording highest accidents and this results in payment of substantial amounts as compensation to accident victims.

Opportunities

- The corporation could do collaborative business with other organisation such as Railways & Tourism Development Corporation, Postal Department/Courier organisations for transporting mail/parcels, etc.
- Scope for designing and implementing special tariff to improve non-peak hour occupancy ratio in buses, which could be patronised by housewives, elderly personnel, etc.
- Scope for catering to multinational corporation (MNC)/Indian companies/enterprises to transport their employees to/from various residential areas to/ from the company officers at special charges.
- Scope for designing and implementing more innovative schemes to motivate employees for higher levels of performance, thereby, reducing manpower cost per unit.

Threats

- Change of policies of state government, which may offer more concessions to bus users, cannot be ruled out, which may improve its profitability.

- Unpredictable escalation of diesel fuel prices to high level as witnessed in 2008, which are beyond the control of the corporation causing reduction in profits and which would warrant increase of bus fares which would he detested by its customers, *viz.*, passengers.
- Possibility of unionism getting stronger, leading perhaps to higher burden of wages, lower staff productivity unless control by deterrent management action.
- Possibility of the government laying down restrictions on land use for development of commercial complexes in vacant land at depots/bus stations.
- Bus fare/traffic revision approvals getting turned down or modified by limiting the fare increase as deemed fit by the government, which may cover only part of the increased of inputs such as materials, wages, etc., leading to increase losses.
- Improved communications networks, as well as adoption of futuristic 'work-from-home' practices gradually reducing need for travelling to work place to some extent, especially in urban areas and metro policies.

Resource Utilisation

Resource: Machines (Buses)

The product marketed by a passenger road transport undertaking like BMTC, is seat-kilometers. Relating to the utilisation of buses, the following data need to be perused, which presents the change and growth across a few key attributes/performance variables.

From Table 5.1, it can be seen that the performance w.r.t utilisation of the main mobile assets, namely vehicles, has been characterised by the following trends:

- *Growth of Fleet*: The fleet has shown a good growth from 3,925 in 2006-07 to 5,111 in 2008-09, a growth of 1,176 buses i.e., an increase of 30 per cent in two years, giving an average percentage increase of 15 per cent per annum (pa), which is considered

Table 5.1

Performance w.r.t. Utilisation

	2006-07	2007-08	2008-09	Change % (2008-09 vs. 2007-08)	
1. No. of Owned buses	3925	4736	5111	375	7.92
2. a) Cancelled Kms per Bus	2588	2371	2385	14	0.59
b) Cancelled Kms per Bus/Day	7.09	6.5	5.53	0.03	0.46
3. Fleet utilisation (%)	94	93.6	94.5	0.9	0.96
4. Vechile utilisation (Kms per bus per day)	231.7	225.37	227.9	2.53	1.12
5. Occupancy ratio (%) (Load Factor–LF)	63.3	63	63.8	08	1.27
6. Passengers Carried per Day (lakhs)	37.75	38.59	40.27	1.68	4.35
7. Break down rate (Per 10,000 kms)	0.09	0.08	0.07	-0.01	-12.5
8. Earnings per km (Paise/Km)	26.62	24.95	24.63	-0.32	-1.28

Source: Compiled from Annual Reports.

quite good. However, the growth in the year 2008-09 was not very significant being only 375 or only 7.9 per cent. Also, viewed from another point of view, on perennially crowded routes in the city, we could provide buses, which can have a (2x2) seat configuration, in which the two-seater on one side could be collapsed either into a single-seater (1 seat), so as to create more open space in the gangway for earring more standing passengers especially in morning and evening hours. This alternative saves the corporation to some extent on the capital expenditure required to purchase buses.

- *Fleet Utilisation (FU)*: This has shown an increase of 0.5 with FU going up to 94.5 per cent during the 2-year period from 2006 to 2007. As this index is indicative of road worthiness of the fleet, and since capital cost of acquiring additional buses is quite high, efforts should be made to attain at least 95 per cent FU, through a good maintenance system.

- *Vehicle Utilisation*: This index, which is akin to plant utilisation in a factory, which tells us the number of kms run by per bus per day, decreased from 231.7 in 2006-07 to 227.9 in 2008-09. It is felt that an increase in VU to about 10 kms pa could be attempted through express long-distance route buses and by extending the crew utilisation to the full span of 8 hours in the crew's shift. There could be practical difficulties on a few routes, but at least on quite a few other routes, such operational strategies could be tried.
- *Occupancy Ratio (%)*: This index has remained consistent at about 63 per cent in 2006-07, growing marginally to 63.8 per cent in 2008-09.

At this level, it implies that there is no overcrowding in the BMTC buses, by ensuring timely addition to the fleet of buses and hence, we could see that convenience of the public travelling has been kept in mind.

Resource: Manpower

- *Manpower Productivity*: This index, indicative of the productive utilisation manpower, works out to be 47.29 in 2006-07, 42.07 in 2007-08 and 43.83 in 2008-09. The year 2006-07, hence, recorded the highest manpower productivity during the period. After a significant drop in 2007-08, it again increased in 2008-09. The low productivity in 2007-08 was on account of substantial increase in total staff during the year from 20,565 to 25,542 or by 4,977, i.e., by as high as 24 per cent, while the total service kms increased from 3334.9 lakh kms to 3,766.85 lakh kms, i.e., by only 12.95 per cent. However, in the next year, kms increased from 3,766.85 to 4,062.43 lakh kms. i.e., by 7.85 per cent, while total staff went up from 25,542 to 27,644 or by only 2,102, i.e., by 8.2 per cent, thereby, almost matching the percentage increase in total service kms, which was not the case in the preceding year 2007-08 in which total staff increased by as much as 24 per cent, but the increase in the product, kilometers operated, increased by only 12.95 per cent.

Staff per Schedule per 100 kms of Vehicle Utilisation (VU)

A new performance index, which is derived by dividing staff per schedule ratio by VU, staff per schedule per 100 kms of VU, is a realistic performance index to gauge manpower productivity. The trend in this index has been shown in Table 5.2.

Table 5.2

Manpower Utilisation

	2006-07	*2007-08*	*2008-09*	*Per cent Change 2008-09 vs. 2007-08*
1. Staff ratio on schedules in operation	4.9	5.4	5.2	-3.7%
2. Staff ration per 100 kms of VU	2.11	2.38	2.28	-4.2%

Source: Compiled from Annual Reports.

The new perormance index, namely, staff ratio per 100 kms of VU has, thus, decreased steadily from 2.38 in 2007-08 to 2.28 in 2008-09. This translates to a reduction by 0.10 or 4.2 per cent, which in turn translates to a saving of ₹ 13.67 crores pa. Of the two ratios, therefore, staff ratio per 100 km of VU enables realistic review of staff per bus per unit productivity, which has resulted in significant savings on staff costs.

The next important resources being deployed by BMTC are the materials, namely:

- Fuel (Diesel).
- Tyres.

The value of fuel (diesel) fluctuated violently in 2006-07 and 2007-08 and has shown a meteoric and violent rise in price, especially, during the period of review and is currently fluctuating around $75-$80 per barrel. For BMTC, the cost per km for these two items was as follows for 2008-09:

- Fuel: 701.8 (per km).
- Tyres: 71.1 (per km).

The efficiency of utilisation of these two resources is gauged by the following indices:

- Fuel: KMPL (kilometer per litre of diesel).
- Tyres: total tyre life in kms.

Fuel

Fuel efficiency in terms of KMPL have shown the following trend. It was 4.58 in 2006-07, 4.45 in 2007-08 and 4.37 in 2008-09. KMPL has, therefore, been decreasing during the three-year period, with the decrease from 2006-07 to 2008-09 being 0.21, which works out to be 4.6 per cent. If the same level of fuel efficiency could be maintained as in 2006-07,this would imply savings in fuel costs to the tune of ₹ 16.46 crore. However, the decline in kmpl could be due to addition of a significant number of Volvo buses for the Valvo and Vajra, and Vayu Vajra services, which run at much higher speeds owing to more powerful engines and, hence, consume more head per km operated.

However, efforts need to be made to improve KMPL, especially, in view of the fact that petroleum crude prices, which had touched an all-time high of about $150 per barrel, could again rise to such levels, though the price of petroleum crude is presently ranging between $75 and $80 per barrel. It has been seen in another comparable state transport corporation such as Andhra Pradesh State Road Transport Corporation (APSRTC), which had engaged a former service engineer of Ashok Leyland, that improvement in kmpl by 0.10 to 0.30 and, hence, significant savings in fuel are possible if drivers are trained to drive at optimal speeds.

Also, BMTC by itself and by combining with other STUs, which are members of ASRTU, Delhi, could also make the two leading passenger bus manufacturers in India, namely, Tata Motors and Ashok Leyland, to supply buses with different diesel engines that are more fuel efficient, and being manufactured in countries like Japan, Korea, etc., such engines would indeed make a substantial difference and improve the fuel efficiency of buses, saving the corporation's crores of rupees.

Tyres

It is seen that tyre life (total) for the years 2006-07, 2007-08 and 2008-09 was respectively 1.64. 1.67 and 1.55 lakh kms, thus, showing a decrease of as much as 12,000 kms per tyre from its peak or a decrease of 7.2 per cent, which amounts to an increase in tyre cost to the tune of ₹ 1.53 crore for the year 2008-09, during which it had incurred a total expenditure of ₹ 21.37 crore.

It is generally seen that total tyre life comes down if the average number of retreads per tyre comes down and this happens mainly due to tyres being run for an extended period in the new stage because of which they become unfit for further retreads and the new tyre has to be scrapped without undergoing further retreads. In the case of BMTC, the average new tyre life has marginally increased steadily from 0.69 to 0.70 and then to 0.73 lakh kms, while the retreaded tyre life decreased from 0.37 to 0.36 lakh kms. This increased usage of tyres for extended life in the new stage has possibly been a reason for total tyre life reduction in the recent years, as mentioned above. What is seen is that, the tyre retreadibility factor (in lakh/km) was 2.59 in 2006-07, increasing to 2.71 in 2007-08 and then decreasing to a rather low figure of 2.33. This has obviously led to tyre life increase in 2007-08, compared to the previous year and a significant decrease from 1.67 in 2007-08 to 1.55 lakh kms in 2008-09 i.e., by 12,000 kms. Efforts could be made to improve tyre maintenance practices, especially, in respect of removal of tyres in time for retreading and not over-running them in the new stage. Owing to which, some of the new tyres worn out and become unfit for being taken up for retreading, which, otherwise, could be done twice or thrice and thus, derive a higher total tyre life. Also, correct inflation pressures in tyres during daily check up must be ensured to avert under inflation, which leads to damage tubes and over inflation which results in concussion bursts of tyres.

Table 5.3 shows the figures of profit, effective kilometers operated and profit per kilometers.

Table 5.3

Financial Performance (Earnings and Cost)

	2006-07 (A)	*2007-08 (B)*	*2008-09 (C)*	*Per cent Increase (C over B)*
Total Earnings (₹ lakh)	88759	93980	100063	6.12
Profit (₹ lakh)	22432	14023	5518	-60.00
Effective Kilometers (lakh kms)	3334	3767	4062	7.83
Profit per km (paise per km)	672	372	136	-63.44

Source: Compiled from Annual Reports.

Table 5.4

Itemised Costs

(₹ Lakhs [paise])

		2006-07 (A)	2007-08 (B)	2008-09 (C)	Per cent to Total Cost
1.	Fuel (Disel)	25104 (753p)	29066 (772p)	35927 (884p)	38
2.	Tyres	1162 (35p)	1670 (44p)	2137 (53p)	2.3
3.	Spare Parts	784 (24p)	1571 (42p)	2198 (54p)	2.3
4.	Reconditioning	699 (21p)	651 (17p)	1488 (37p)	1.6
5.	MV Tax	3891 (117p)	4408 (120p)	4491 (123p)	4.8
6.	Depreciation	5673 (170p)	6757 (180p)	9766 (240p)	10.3
7.	Staff Costs	21228 (637p)	28228 (749p)	32505 (800p)	34.3
8.	Overheads	2934 (88p)	3813 (101p)	2779 (68p)	2.9
	Total Cost	66327 (1990p)	79958 (2400p)	94545 (2836p)	100

Source: Compiled from Annual Reports.

Earnings/Revenue

It is seen from Table 5.3 that earnings have grown by 6.12 per cent in 2008-09, compared to the previous year. The effective kms have also taken a jump to 7.83 per cent during 2008-09. However, the profit for the year decreased from ₹ 140.23 crore to ₹ 55.18 crore—a decrease of as much as 60 per cent. The profit per km (PPK) decreased from 372 to 132 paise (p) per km—a drop of 63.44 per cent. It may be worthy to mention herein the commendable efforts of BMTC in the recent times about the numerous commercial projects being planned and executed to get revenue through lease of commercially built complexes and malls such as Shantinagar, Jaynagar, Koramangala, Banashankari, etc. Such projects are of two kinds, the first being those under Jawaharlal Nehru National Urban Renewal Mission (JNNURM) scheme, which BMTC is getting substantial funding from Central/State Government, and the second one in which the corporation has initiated build, operate, transfer (BOT) kind of commercial infrastructure projects on its own through public private partnership (PPP) mode.

Itemised Costs

The following are the reasons for the decrease in profitability:

- *Fuel cost*: Increase from 772 p to 884 p, or by 112 p. i.e., 14.5 per cent is due mainly to drop in kmpl from 4.45 in the previous year to 4.37 in 2008-09.

- *Staff Cost*: Increased from 749 p to 800 p i.e., 6.8 per cent.
- *Depreciation Cost*: Shot up from 180 p to as high as 240 p, an increase of as much as 33.3 per cent, which indicates a significantly overprovided depreciation fund in this year compared to previous two years.
- *Tyre Cost*: Increased from 44 p to 53 p, an increase of about 20.5 per cent, also a substantial, which was due mainly to a reduction in average life of tyres by as much as 12,000 kms per tyre, which warrants better maintenance and use of tyres.
- *MVTax*: Increased only marginally from 120 p to 123 p.
- *Spare Parts Cost*: Also, increased significantly from 42 p in the previous year to 54 p in 2008-09, an increase of 29 per cent, which is partly owing to more and more Volvo AC coaches being added to the fleet.
- Overhead Costs: Decreased appreciably from as high as 101 p to only 68 p, a reduction of as much as 48.5 per cent, which indeed deserves commendation in as much as this head of cost is a controllable cost, which is ignored in many public sector enterprises.

Total Cost: The overall result of the aforesaid changes in cost as an increase in total cost from 2400 p to 2836 p, i.e., by 436 p or ₹ 4.36p, or by about 18.2 per cent, which is quite significant and has led to a decline in profits for the corporation.

Of the said increase in cost, depreciation for the year constituted an increase by as much as 60 p per km as mentioned in the 3rd bullet point, above. The corporation, however, still obtained a profit to the tune of ₹ 55.18 crores, despite enhanced depreciation expense of ₹ 30.09 crore for the year 2008-09.

Decision-Information Matrix (DIM)

It was found during discussions with the managing director, the directors/heads of department that BMTC is on the move and has become commercially quite aggressive. Under such present management culture, the hands of the top management team would indeed get further strengthened by developing an improvised management information system (MIS) through a 'Decision Information Matrix (DIM).' A specimen of information content required for a typical decision under the DIM format is presented Table 5.5.

Table 5.5

Proposed Decision Information Matrix (DIM)

Decision Domain	*Decision to be made*	*Decision type (Routine/Non-routine)*	*Data/Information Content requried*
Operations	New Route to be started	Non-routine	Statistical data of origin, destination places and places/towns/villages along the route, new factories or developments planned in the area, statistical data from government departments, data on private buses, trains playing, quality of roads along the route, nature of traffic demand (whether personal or seasonal, etc.).
Operations	Augmentation of Buses on	Routine	Total number of buses, route length, average vehicle utilisation, average a earning per kilometre in paise (EPKM) and occupancy ratio (OR), avg. profit per km, number of private vehicles/FPT vehicles (jeeps, autorickshaws, private vans, contract carriages, etc., operation along the full length of parts of the route. Additional data/information Requried: – List of competing routes also needing augmentation through additional buses with the information/data as listed above. – Newly originated commercial activities along the route. – List of public representatives or public. – Representations pending for the route. – Social facts warranting augmentation.

Source: Compiled from Annual Reports.

It is said that development of such a DIM would streamline the MIS towards the decision-making needs of the top management.

Even external environment related information would need to be gathered and provided in DIM, wherever necessary, such as in case of governments plans to construct new colonies or new towns (such as the Navi Mumbai townships in Mumbai, forecasted demand for two wheelers and four wheelers adopted by automobile manufacturers in their production plans, etc.

Stakeholders' Concerns

This section presents the aspects relating to various stakeholders, namely, government, society, commuters and employees.

Government

The government's primary concerns are the provisions of efficient and satisfactory transport services to commuters. At the same time, the government would want BMTC to provide the services without incurring any losses and bringing a burden to the state. Hence, BMTC would require to continue to have, under the existing system, regular performance monitoring of provision of adequate number of buses on different routes with reasonably acceptable frequency to take care of passengers needs in the city and its suburbs, which have grown rapidly and house large residential colonies. The government would also urge BMTC to ensure safety of lives of passengers as well as road users. In this context, it is seen that the rate of accidents i.e., number of accidents per one lakh kms operated by BMTC has been hovering in the range of 0.14 to 0.16 in the last three years and has not been reduced, being 0.15. In 2008-09, amongst the accidents, fatal ones involving loss of precious lives need to be reduced.

Drivers' training on driving simulators is to be adopted in order to ensure that the drivers attitudes are oriented more towards safety of lives. It is heartening to note that KSRTC has been training drivers on computer-based simulators for the past few years. These efforts will surely pay off in the long run and will in few years reduce the compensation paid by BMTC for deaths. Yet, another concern of the government could be the creations of jobs. BMTC keeps recruiting manpower mostly for productive categories, such as driver and conductors but it has reduced its man power over all to very competitive levels. Its staff ratio on schedules is one of the lowest among large STUs in India, having been brought down progressively from

6.22 in 1996-97 to as low as 4.79 in 2007-08. This was necessary to make the corporation earn profits and to offset the raising cost of inputs such as fuel, tyres, staff wages, etc. Hence, if BMTC has to satisfy the twin objectives of the government, namely, adequate and efficient transport as well as generation of employment, it could do so without impairing its financial position and profits i.e., through growth of its fleet of buses year after year. It is seen that in the last year under review i.e., 2007-08, BMTC's fleet increased from 4,819 to 5,502 i.e., by 683 buses or by about 14 per cent, which is indeed a very healthy and adequate growth rate, especially keeping in view that in doing so, its occupancy per bus (load factor) has not fallen, but on the contrary has risen from 70.2 per cent to 72.2 per cent during the period. As regards number of staff on rolls, the figure has increased from 20,565 in 2006-07 to 27,644 in 2008-09, with increase in staff ratio from a low of 4.9 to 5.2 in 2008-09, which is a negative trend in productivity and performance and this has also led to an increase in expenditure on staff wages.

Thus, apparently, BMTC has succeeded in satisfying the various objectives of the government, especially in respect of employment generation, while improving its profits that have gone up from ₹ 26.70 crore in 2001-02 to ₹ 55.18 crore in 2008-09.

Society

The society's concerns with reference to BMTC would be improvement in number of buses put into operation and their growth, provision of adequate amenities in bus station, provision of employee opportunities, reduction of pollution and reduction in number of breakdowns and accidents. As mentioned earlier, BMTC has accomplished a very good growth in buses operated as well as in provision of employment. However, reduction in rate of accidents is yet to be accomplished to acceptable levels, since the rate is range-bound between 0.14 to 0.6 in the last 3 years. In regard to breakdown rate, the figure had come down from as high as 0.19 in 2001-02 to as low as 0.07 per 10,000 kms by 2008-09. The rate of breakdown ought to have come down to 0.07, since new buses are being added more in the recent years. Perhaps tackling the 'A class' items of breakdowns would enable reduction of the overall breakdown rates still further.

Commuters

The commuters concerns normally are growth in fleet operated on the various routes, yielding higher frequency and reduced waiting time, facilities in availing services such as reservation of bus seats for travel, bus passes, making representations, accessing information on services, etc., through website, as well as appropriate electronic display systems at bus stations, etc. Growth in fleet has been quite satisfactory as discussed earlier. On the latter aspect of access of services, information, etc., a special mention must be made about the following initiatives taken by BMTC.

IT Initiatives of BMTC to Facilitate Commuters

Amongst the IT initiatives taken by BMTC, the following are worth mentioning.

- Electronic Ticketing Machines (ETMs) in buses, which make the process more transparent, providing additional data on passenger travel patterns, etc., information on minimising scope for fraud, etc.
- Computerised depot management system at all depots that has not only given savings on manpower but rich database for decision-making.
- Automatic Daily Pass Vending Machine at bus station has been installed for the convenience of passengers.
- Global positioning system/general packet radio service (GPS/GPRS) based Automatic Vehicle Location and Real Time Passenger Information System, which is now implemented for about 10 per cent of its fleet and will be scaled up. However, for such a technology—intensive project, both the central and the state government must extend adequate financial grants to state transport undertakings (STUs), which are also capital intensive, which STUs can ill afford but which are going to even improve their financial performances.

But, what could now give added advantage, both in information display and in earning commercial revenue for the corporation, is the installation of electronic display boards at various bus stops to disseminate information on expected time of arrivals of buses with scope to intermittently display commercial ads, by breaking the timings display for ads for just about 5 seconds on and off.

Employees

Their stake concerns wages commensurate with the rise in cost of living, protection of jobs, compensation for higher productivity, etc. It is seen that the corporation has been carrying out periodic wage revision and compensating them for rise in cost of living through dearness allowance (DA) revision. Even jobs are much better protected, than under the private sector, except with employees losing their jobs on grounds of serious misconduct, monetary fraud, corruption, etc.

Recommendations

BMTC has emerged as a state transport corporation with tremendous dynamism and good growth in the last three years and is now being reckoned as a leader amongst India's STUs. It leads in most aspects not only amongst urban, but also amongst all STUs in India. It has also been swift in adopting state-of-the-art technology and information technology (IT), in scaling up BOT and other projects. Under JNNURM scheme, a provision of comfortable as well as market segment oriented bus services was approved. The organisation structure and associated delegation of authority seem to be delivering the results as of now. However, there is a need to design a decision-oriented MIS, in order to make decisions yet more effective and profit oriented. An MIS with DIM could be designed without much difficulty as has been the case of in other STUs. The following recommendations are made, which will go to boost BMTC's performance to much higher levels and will safeguard the interests of the stakeholders namely, commuters for improved, safe and punctual services, society for less polluting buses to conserve the environment, as well as sufficiency of buses for more frequent buses. Through increased profitability, BMTC was targeting growth in employment generation, increasing state revenues, taxes, better salaries; and to meet growing competition from private transporters and other modes such as auto rickshaws have adapted the following strategies:

- Developing new information outputs such as vehicle-wise, service-wise and route-wise profitability statements, exception reports on low performing units, routes, services, crew and mechanics with more enriched and decision relevant information/data content.
- Streamlining the set of indices of performance being presently deployed for performance review in Bayerische Motoren Werke AG (BMW).
- Scaling up the GPS project to all BMTC's buses, as it benefits passengers with real time information on arrival of buses. Also, the LED display boards at bus stops in city and even suburban/mofussil bus stops could fetch lot of revenue through intermittent display of ads on a commercial basis. The real time display of accurate information of bus arrivals at bus stop will give confidence to people waiting at bus stops who will then refrain from getting into an auto, waiting to grab customers.
- Reducing accidents through Driving Simulator deployment at a larger scale, as these help in inculcating the correct psyche in drivers for accident avoidance and road safety and, thus, in developing an attitude for safe driving.
- Training depot managers in all regions, head office to use the concept of 'Opportunity Costs' wherever possible, so that they take decisions controlling the costs.
- Initiatiating BOT projects even by demolishing depots and accommodating them in beg ground floor of the new multistorey structure, deploying the higher floor level spaces for commercial purposes.
- Applying the concept of 'Strategic Business Units' and, thus, aim at improving their performance through a 'quantum jump' approach rather than an 'incremental growth' approach.
- Training all managers on the method of forecasting the depot's month end profit from day-to-day or at least from week-to-week within the current month itself, so that there is still some time of a few days left in the month to cause corrective action to improve the depot's performance, before the month ends.

- Training maintenance mechanics on concepts of quality in maintenance and upkeep of buses, especially the ones which cater to higher income segments that demand classy and good quality services.

The author had developed a method for a large STU, which like BMTC, has all depots with extensively computerised systems in operations, maintenance, stores, personnel and accounts sections of the depot. Such a system will transform the mindsets of the Depot/Divisional Managers into proactive rather than reactive.

6 Hubli Electricity Supply Company Limited

S.K. Mathur

Introduction

Hubli Electricity Supply Company (HESCOM) was incorporated on April 30, 2002, and commenced its business from June 1, 2002. The company is primarily engaged in the business of distribution of electricity in the district of Dharwad, Gadag, Belgum, Haveri, Uttara Kannada, Bagalkot and Bijapur. There are two operation and maintenance (O&M) zones namely, Hubly zones and Belgum Zone. Hubli zone covers one O&M circle with head quarters at Hubli, covering six O&M divisions located at Hubli, Dharwad, Gadag, Haveri, Sirsi and Karwar.

Belgum zone covers two O&M circle. Bijapur, Belgum, Ghataprabha, Bailhongal and Chikkodi O&M divisions come within the jurisdiction of Belgum Circle. Bijpur, Bagalkot and Jamkandi O&M Divisions come under the purview of Bijapur circle. There are 62 O&M sub-divisions in the HESCOM jurisdiction. The year 2004-05, being the third year of operation, was a challenging year for the company. The company took various initiatives in tune with the policy objectives of Government of Karnataka (GoK) to bring about efficiency in the power sector, especially in the field of distribution of electricity and providing better service to the customers. The company is primarily engaged in the business of distribution of electricity with operations in the districts of Dharwad, Gadag, Belgaum, Haveri, Uttar, Kannada, Bagalkot and Bijapur.

Strategies and Vision of the Company

- Enhancement of revenue generation.
- Strengthening and refurbishing distribution network to reduce losses and cost of operation.

- Enhancing employee productivity.
- Providing best services to its consumers.

HESCOM's Vision

- 100 per cent rural electrification.
- Reduce transmission and distribution (T&D) losses to 22 per cent.
- 100 per cent metering.
- Elimination of low voltage pockets.
- Reduction in interruptions.
- Power supply on demand.
- Eliminate commercial losses.
- Application of information technology (IT) in more and more activities.

Collection Efficiency

During 2008-09, collection efficiency of the company has increased to 89.0 per cent from 80.63 per cent as compared to 2007-08. The category-wise collection efficiency can be seen from Table 6.1 and Figure 6.1.

Table 6.1

Collection Efficiency

Category	*Collection Efficiency (in %)*				
	2008-09	*2007-08*	*2006-07*	*2005-06*	*2004-05*
LT1BJ/KJ	80.00	77.52	4.59	8.1	12.93
LT2	102.54	104.28	101.09	90.55	89.36
LT3	102.18	102.61	100.64	99.91	97.17
LT4IP	62.21	8.87	11.34	9.33	11.85
LT5	98.12	101.19	101.05	101.18	98.03
LT6W/s & P/L	112.35	66.11	88.15	61.89	48.87
LT7	99.43	104.06	101.7	100.41	106.61
HT	95.80	98.23	110.36	92.43	95.70
Misc	38.61	36.51	54.60	33.60	15.68
Total	88.90	80.63	87.02	73.03	75.40

Source: Compiled from Annual Reports.

Figure 6.1

Collection Efficiency during the Period 2003-04 to 2008-09

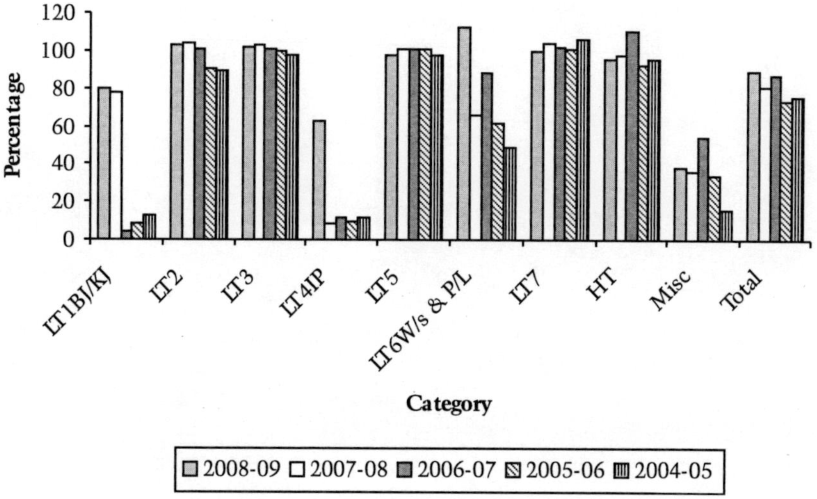

Source: Compiled from Annual Reports.

Energy Sale

The percentage of energy sale for the period 2008-09 to 2003-04 is given in Table 6.2 and Figure 6.2.

Table 6.2

Category-wise Energy Sale during the Period 2004-05 to 2008-09

Category	*Category-wise Energy Sale (in %)*				
	2008-09	*2007-08*	*2006-07*	*2005-06*	*2004-05*
LT1BJ/KJ	2.40	2	2	1	2
LT2	14.85	15	14	15	15
LT3	3.73	4	3	3	3
LT4IP	53.94	54	58	57	58
LT5	4.82	5	5	5	5
LT6W/s & P/L	4.05	4	4	4	5
LT7	0.19	0	0	0	0
HT	16.02	16	15	14	12

Source: Compiled from Annual Reports.

Figure 6.2

Category-wise Energy Sale (in %) during the Period 2004-05 to 2008-09

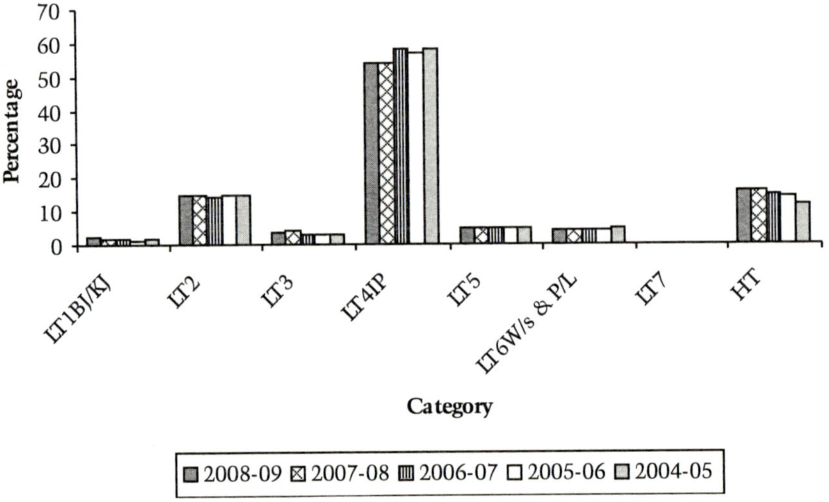

Source: Compiled from Annual Reports.

Customer Profile

The company had a customer base of 30.99 lakh at the beginning of the year. With the addition of 1.56 lakh new consumers during the year, the customer base has increased to 32.55 lakh, as at the end of the year March 31, 2009. This is clearly explained in Table 6.3 and Figure 6.3.

Table 6.3

Customer Base with respect to Consumption

Years	*Customer Base (Installations in Nos)*
2004-05	27.70
2005-06	28.61
2006-07	29.23
2007-08	30.99
2008-09	32.55

Source: Compiled from Annual Reports.

Figure 6.3

Customer Base with respect to Consumption

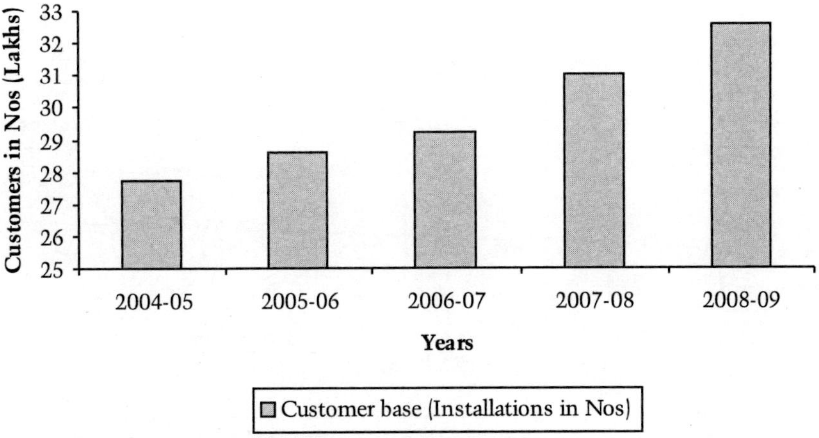

Source: Compiled from Annual Reports.

Table 6.4

Revenue Demand and Collection

(₹ in crore)

Years	*Revenue Demand*	*Revenue Collection*
2004-05	958.76	752.10
2005-06	1076.49	786.13
2006-07	1120.51	975.05
2007-08	1237.82	998.10
2008-09	1354.95	1204.69

Source: Compiled from Annual Reports.

Figure 6.4

Customer Base with respect to Consumption (Revenue)

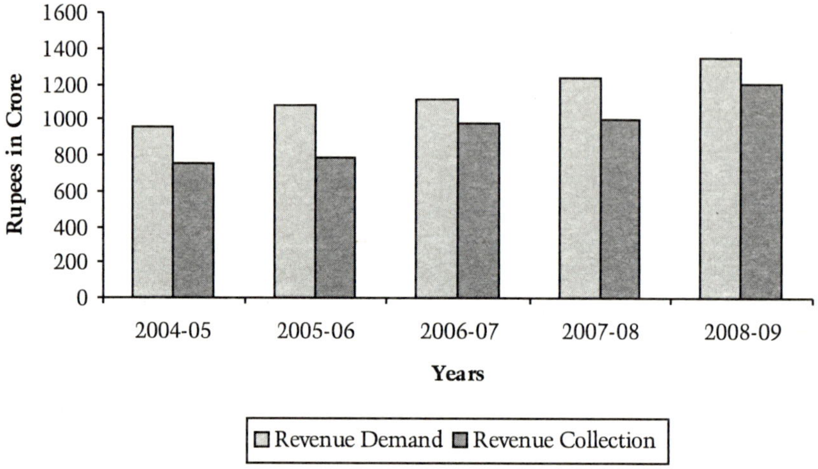

Source: Compiled from Annual Reports.

Bulk Purchase Power in HESCOM

As per GoK Notification dated July 6, 2005, the allocation of power from conventional energy sources is at 20.35 per cent [including Hukeri Rural Electric Cooperative Society (HRECS) at 0.5009%] and non-conventional energy projects are allocated, based on geographical area of HESCOM. This allocation has been revised by GoI, vide its notificated dated, December 28, 2005. The share of major independent power producers (IPPs), Karnataka Power Corporation Ltd. (KPCL), Raichur Termal Power Station 4 (RTPS-4) and Yelahanka DGS has been removed from HESCOM and share of Sharavathy Generation Station was increased to 25.67 per cent. GoK has revised the allocation of Sharavathy Generating Station and RTPS of M/s KPCL in respect of HESCOM, vide its notification dated April 22, 2006, in Table 7.5.

The power purchase as per GoK notification dated April 22, 2006, has been billed for financial year 2009. The total energy purchased, the actual energy drawn at interface point and cost thereon are shown in Table 7.6.

During the financial year 2008-09, due to acute shortage of power in Karnataka, GoK decided to purchase power from IPPs and co-generation

Table 6.5

Allocation of Sharavathy Generating Station and RTPS

Source	*HESCOM Share (%)*
Sharavathy	25.67
RTPS 1&2	20.36
RTPS 3	3.63
RTPS 4	-
RTPS 5 &6	20.36
RTPS 7	20.35

Source: Compiled from Annual Reports.

Table 6.6

Details of Power Purchased by GoK

Total Energy Purchased in MUs	*Total Energy drawn at interface points in MUs*	*Power Purchase Cost in Crores*	*Average Power Purchase Cost (₹ per unit)*	
			At Generation Point	*At Interface Point*
8175.96	7504.57	1925.94	2.40	2.57

Source: Compiled from Annual Reports.

sugar plants at the rate of ₹ 7.25 in December 2008 and ₹ 6.50/unit from January 2009 to March 2009. The energy purchased from these generators (co-generation) from December 2008 to March 2009 is 217.19 MU, at an average cost of ₹ 6.66/unit.

For prompt and early payments, as per rebate scheme in Power Purchase Agreement (PPA) and Central Electricity Regulatory Commission (CERC) order, HESCOM has availed rebate of ₹ 6.17 crore during financial year 2008-09 from central generating stations, including PGCIL; 393.97 MU of energy has been purchased under unscheduled interchange mechanism, under inter availability based tariff (ABT) at the payment of ₹ 215.46 crore.

HESCOM purchases power from KPCL and IPPs at the tariff fixed by the Karnataka Electricity Regulatory Commission (KERC) from time to time. The average cost of energy purchase is ₹ 4.22 pu during financial year 2008-09. As per GoK order dated, May 10, 2005, HESCOM has paid SPPCC/PCKL administrative expenses amounting to ₹ 0.59 crore.

Distribution Losses

During the year, the distribution loss of the company stood at 24.96 per cent as against 25.06 per cent in the preceding year. The details are given in Table 6.7.

Table 6.7

Distribution Losses

S. No.	*Particulars*	*2008-09*	*2007-08*	*2006-07*
1.	Total energy available for sale	7367.35	7075.69	7257.36
2.	Total metered sales	2653.09	2445.52	2233.10
3.	Total unmetered sales	2875.62	2856.21	3005.31
4.	Total sales	5528.71	5302.74	5238.42
5.	Distribution losses	1838.64	1772.95	2018.94
6.	Percentage of distribution losses	24.96%	25.06%	27.82%

Source: Compiled from Annual Reports.

Reduction of Distribution Losses

HESCOM has initiated several measures to improve its internal systems and commercial operations during the year. Some of the measures are listed below:

- Reconductoring of 11/33 KV lines with higher capacity conductor.
- Establishing new sub-stations to avoid lengthy 33 KV lines and overloading of sub-stations.
- Providing additional power transformers to avoid overloading of existing power transformers.
- Providing rural load management system (RLMS) facility to rural feeders.
- Targeting 100 per cent meter reading and billing.
- Timely opening of test reports.
- Providing better quality meters.
- Replacement of meter not recording (MNR) meters.
- Periodical rating and calibration of meters.
- Speedy disposal of pending applications.
- Detection of theft and pilferage.
- Improvement in distribution network.

Financial Performance

Capital Structure

As at the close of March 31, 2009, the paid-up capital of the Corporation stood at ₹ 233.00 crore. The capital structure of the company for the last 6 years is constant and it is shown through Figure 6.5.

Figure 6.5

Capital Structure

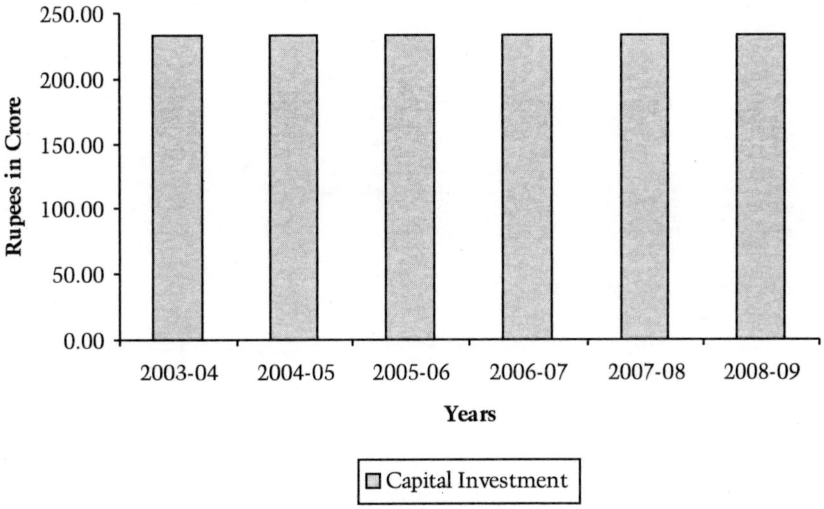

Source: Compiled from Annual Reports.

Reserves and Surplus

The reserves and surplus accumulated upto March 31, 2009, was ₹ -11.09 crore as against ₹ 63.79 crore as on March 31, 2008, respectively. The reserves and surplus of the company for the last 6 years is shown through Figure 6.6. After 2004-05 the company has experienced a negative reserves and surplus due to the decrease in profits. Moreover, the contributions, grants and subsides towards cost of capital assets was also not given during the years.

Figure 6.6

Reserves and Surplus

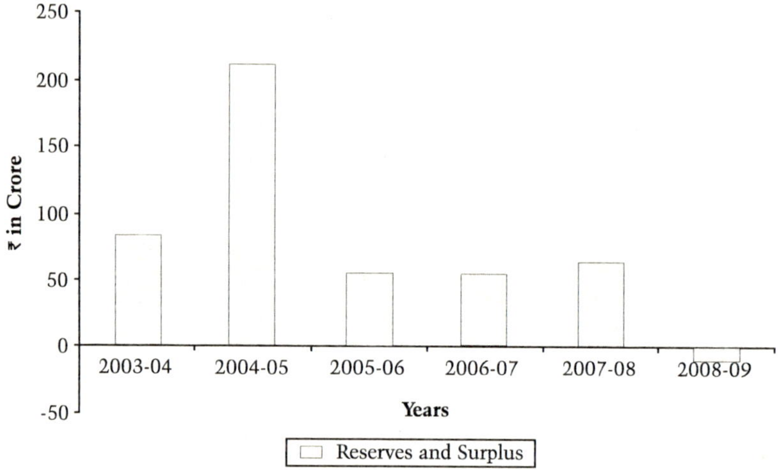

Source: Compiled from Annual Reports.

Profit Before Interest and Taxes

The company profit has not showed a remarkable progress over the years 2003-04 to 2007-08. The year 2008-09 had experienced losses. This is clearly explained through Figure 6.7.

Figure 6.7

Profit Before Interest and Taxes

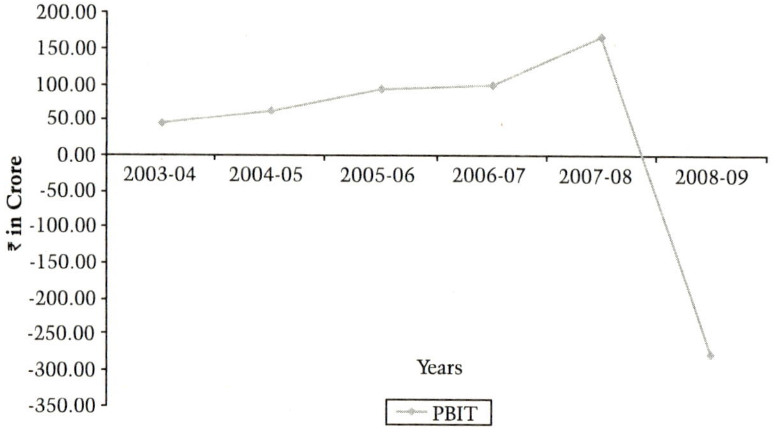

Source: Compiled from Annual Reports.

Liquidity Ratios

Liquidity ratios measure the corporation's ability to meet current obligations. The two ratios *viz.*, current ratio and quick ratio are analysed here. The current ratio is a measure of the corporate short-term solvency. It indicates the availability of current assets in rupees for every one rupee of current liability. A ratio greater than one means that the corporation has more current assets than current liabilities. During the years 2003-04 and 2008-09, the current ratio was good. The company was having more current assets than current liabilities. But it is not always suggestible to have more liquidity. This is clearly explained in Table 6.8 and Figure 6.8.

Table 6.8

Current Ratio

Years	*Current Assets*	*Current Liabilities*	*Current Ratio*
2003-04	940.50	1067.90	88.07
2004-05	1325.90	863.83	153.49
2005-06	1466.78	987.64	148.51
2006-07	1678.14	914.05	183.59
2007-08	1932.73	1080.63	178.85
2008-09	1952.68	1551.10	125.89

Source: Compiled from Annual Reports.

Figure 6.8

Current Ratio

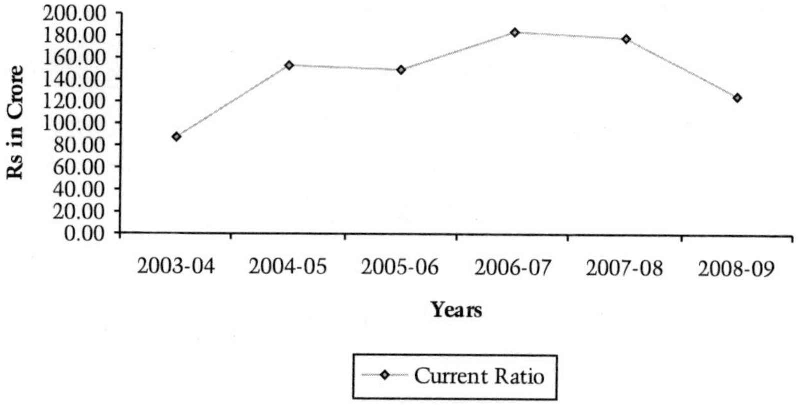

Source: Compiled from Annual Reports.

Leverage Ratios

Leverage ratios show the proportions of debt and equity in financing the firm's assets. It is clear from Table 6.9 that the lenders contribution is less than one rupee, if the owners contribution is one rupee. It is only during the years 2004-05 to 2006-07 that the lenders contribution is more than one rupee of owner's contribution. Debt equity ratio was directly computed by dividing total debt by net worth. The debt equity ratio of the company moved from 1.17:1 in 2003-04 to 6.89:1 in 2008-09.

Table 6.9

Debt/Equity Ratio

Years	*Debt/ Equity*
2003-04	1.17
2004-05	1.69
2005-06	2.79
2006-07	3.69
2007-08	4.87
2008-09	6.89

Source: Compiled from Annual Reports.

Figure 6.9

Debt-Equity Ratio

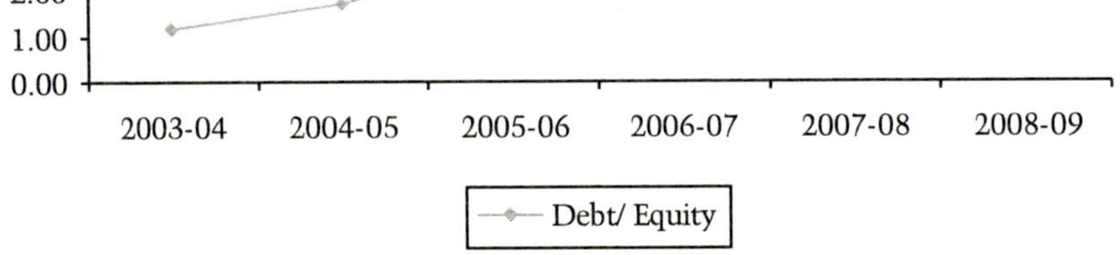

Source: Compiled from Annual Reports.

Return on Sales (ROS) Ratio

This ratio is widely used to evaluate an enterprises operational efficiency. ROS is also known as a firm's 'operating profit margin.' It is calculated using the formula Profit Before Depreciation Interest and Taxes/ Sales. This measure is helpful to management and provides an insight into how much profit is being produced per rupee of sales. As with many ratios, it is best to compare the enterprise's ROS over time to look for trends, and also compare it with similar public enterprises (PEs). An increasing ROS indicates the enterprise is growing more efficient, while a decreasing ROS could signal looming financial troubles. The company experienced a good ROS till 2007-08 but in the year 2008-09 due to the fluctuations in power tariff the company experienced a decrease in ROS.

Figure 6.10

Return on Sales (ROS) Ratio

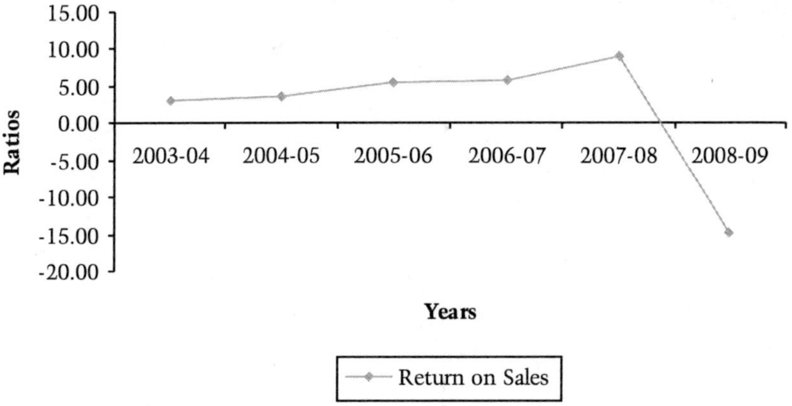

Return on Assets (ROA) Ratio

Return on assets is an indicator of how profitable an enterprise is relative to its total assets. ROA gives an idea as to how efficient management is at using its assets to generate earnings. Calculated by dividing an enterprise's annual earnings by its total assets, ROA is displayed as a percentage. Sometimes this is referred to as 'return on investment.' ROA explains the earnings that were generated from invested capital (assets). ROA for public companies can vary substantially and will be highly dependent on the industry. This is why when using ROA as a comparative measure, it is best to compare it against the enterprise's previous ROA numbers or the ROA of a similar enterprise. The assets of the enterprise comprises both debt and equity. Both of these types of financing are used to fund the operations of the enterprise. The ROA figure gives investors an idea of how effectively the enterprise is converting the money it has to invest into net income. The higher the ROA better the enterprise earning i.e., more money on less investment. This ROA has experienced a drastic fall after 2007-08.

Figure 6.11

Return on Assets (ROA) Ratio

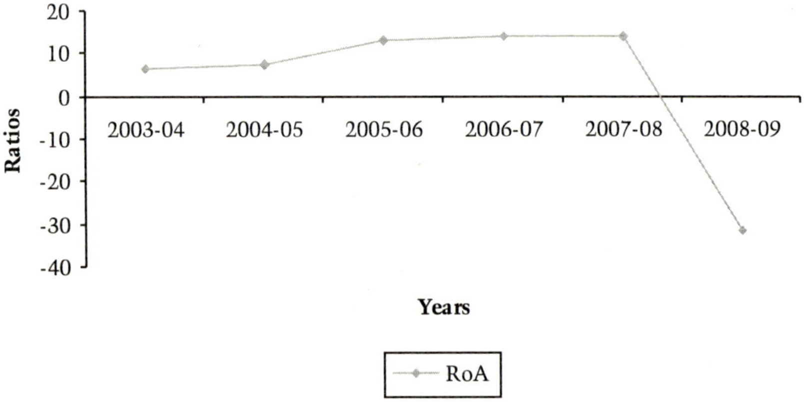

Source: Compiled from Annual Reports.

Return on Equity (ROE) Ratio

Return on equity is a measure of the profitability that reveals how much profit the enterprise is generating with the money that shareholders have invested. ROE is useful for comparing the profitability of an enterprise with that of other firms in the same industry. Figure 6.12 shows that the ROE is at its highest during the years 2007-08 and it has experienced a sudden decline in progress during 2008-09.

Figure 6.12

Return on Equity

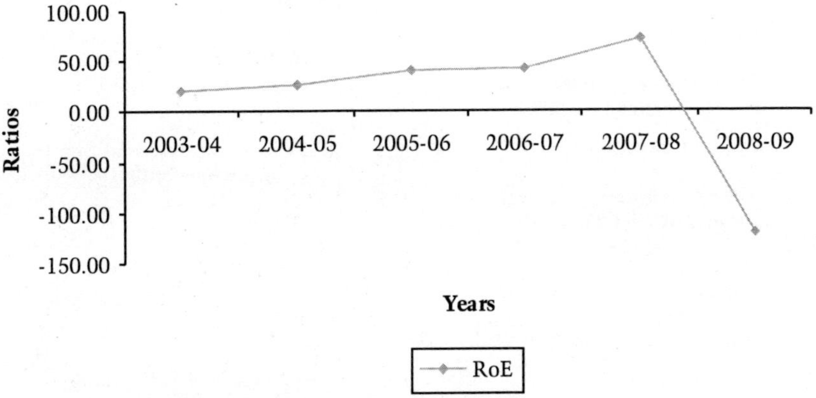

Source: Compiled from Annual Reports.

Table 6.10

Profitability Ratios

	ROS	*ROA*	*ROE*
2003-04	2.96	6.56	19.90
2004-05	3.49	7.51	26.60
2005-06	5.61	12.99	40.39
2006-07	5.68	13.94	42.26
2007-08	8.93	13.98	71.80
2008-09	-14.83	-31.78	-119.57

Source: Compiled from Annual Reports.

Table 6.11

SWOT Analysis

Strengths	*Opportunities*
1. Monopoly in business. 2. The company has huge network for distribution of power. 3. Good infrastructure facilities. 4. The company has got better human resource i.e., around 6,000 employees in various caders to cater to the needs of the public. 5. The company is identifying the areas and deputing the work force for training for the enrichment of the skills.	1. The company shall create special caders for increasing the motivation of the staff on job rotate basis. 2. By motivating the workforce the company could get better returns
Weakness	*Threats*
1. The major weakness of the company is that the pricing policy is not in the hands of the company. 2. As far as the collection of bills are concerned, the company could realise an amount of 60 per cent of the bill from rural local bodies. (still rural bodies owe to the company around 190 crores as of December 31, 2009). 3. The material management and procurement of materials have to be further strengthened.	1. Vigilance activity should be strengthened for arresting the leakages of the power and materials etc. However, the company has got 1 SP, 4 DSPs and 7 circle inspectors on deputation from GoK. 2. Financial wing of the company should be strengthened and also efforts shall be made for enrichment of the skills of the staff by sending them for suitable training. 3. Since there is no lateral movement for the staff of the company between the wings, the morality of the workforce is effected. Hence, steps are to be taken for improvement.

7 Karnataka Neeravari Nigam Ltd.

J. Kiranmai and A. Pawan Kumar

Introduction

Irrigation is an artificial application of water to the soil. It is usually used to assist the growing of crops in dry areas and during periods of inadequate rainfall. Additionally, irrigation also has a few other uses in crop production, which include protecting plants against frost, suppressing weed growing in grain fields and helping in preventing soil consolidation. In contrast, agriculture that relies only on direct rainfall is referred to as rain-fed farming. Irrigation is often studied together with drainage, which is the natural or artificial removal of surface and sub-surface water from a given area. World oceans cover about three-fourth of earth's surface. According to the UN estimates, the total amount of water on the earth is about 1,400 million cubic kilometre, which is enough to cover the earth with a layer of 3,000 meters depth. However, the fresh water constitutes a very small proportion of this enormous quantity. About 2.7 per cent of the total water available on the earth is fresh water of which about 75.2 per cent lies frozen in polar regions and another 22.6 per cent is present as ground water. The rest is available in lakes, rivers, atmosphere, moisture, soil and vegetation. What is effectively available for consumption and other uses is a small proportion of the quantity available in rivers, lakes and ground water. The crisis about water resources development and management, thus, arises because most of the water is not available for use and secondly, it is characterised by its highly uneven spatial distribution. Accordingly, the importance of water has been recognised and greater emphasis is being laid on its economic use and better management. Water on the earth is in motion through the hydrological cycle. The utilisation of water for most of the users i.e., human, animal or plant, involve movement of water. The dynamic and renewable nature of the water resources and the recurrent need for its utilisation requires that water resources are measured in terms of its flow rates. Thus, water resources have two facets. The dynamic resource measured as flow is more relevant for most of developmental needs. The static or fixed nature of the reserve, involving the quantity of water, the length of area of the water bodies, is also relevant for some activities like pisciculture, navigation, etc. Both these aspects are discussed below.

Classification of Irrigation Project

The irrigation projects are classified under three categories, as indicated below depending upon the extent of culturable command area (CCA).

Table 7.1

Irrigation Project

SL.No.	*Category*	*Extent of CCA*
1.	Major irrigation projects	Those having CCA of 10,000 ha or more
2.	Medium irrigation projects	Those having CCA between 2,000 ha to 10,000 ha
3.	Minor irrigation projects	Those having CCA of 2,000 ha or less

Source: Compiled from Annual Reports.

A broad assessment of the area that can be ultimately brought under irrigation, both by surface and ground water, made by the various states in 1960s has indicated that ultimate irrigation potential of the country would be of the order of 113 m.ha. However, the ultimate potential is 139 m.ha, the increase being primarily due to upward revision in assessed potential of minor ground water schemes and minor surface water schemes to 64 m.ha and 17 m.ha, respectively. Minor irrigation projects have both surface and ground water as their source, while major and medium projects mostly exploit surface water resources.

Irrigation: International Scenario

Analysing the country-wise geographical area, arable land and irrigated area in the world, it is found that among the continents, largest geographical area lies in the Africa, which is about 23 per cent of the world geographic area. However, Asia (excluding erstwhile countries of USSR) with only 21 per cent of world geographical area has about 32 per cent of world's arable land followed by North Central America having about 20 per cent of world's arable land. Africa has only 12 per cent of world's arable land. It has been seen that irrigated area in the world has about 18.5 per cent of the arable land in 1994. In 1989, 63 per cent of world's irrigated area was in Asia, whereas in 1994 this percentage has gone up to 64 per cent. Also, 37 per cent of arable land of Asia was irrigated in 1994. Among Asian countries, India has the largest arable land, which is close to 39 per cent of Asia's arable land. Only the USA has more arable land than India.

Water and Constitution of India

India is union of states. The constitutional provisions in respect of allocation of responsibilities between the state and centre fall into three categories: the Union List (List I), the State List (List II) and the Concurrent List (List III). Article 246 of the Constitution deals with subject matter of laws to be made by Parliament and by Legislature of the states. As most of the rivers in the country are inter-state, the regulation and development of waters of these rivers is a source of inter-state differences and disputes. In the Constitution, water is a matter included in Entry 17 of List II i.e., State List. This entry is subject to the provision of Entry 56 of List I i.e., Union List.

Article 246

- Notwithstanding anything in clauses (2) and (3), Parliament has exclusive power to make laws with respect to any of the matters enumerated in List I in the seventh schedule (in this Constitution referred to as the 'Union List').
- Notwithstanding anything in clause (3), Parliament, and, subject to clause (1), the legislature of any state also, have power to make laws with respect to any of the matters enumerated in List III in the Seventh Schedule (in this, Constitution referred to as the 'Concurrent List').
- Subject to clauses (1) and (2), the legislature of any state has exclusive power to make laws for such state or any part thereof with respect to any of the matters enumerated in List II in the

Seventh Schedule (in this, Constitution referred to as the 'State List').

- Parliament has power to make laws with respect to any matter for any part of the territory of India not included in a state notwithstanding that such matter is a matter enumerated in the State List.

Article 262

In case of disputes relating to waters, Article 262 provides:

- Parliament may by law provide for the adjudication of any dispute or complaint with respect to the use, distribution or control of the waters of, or in, any inter-state river or river valley.
- Notwithstanding anything in this Constitution, Parliament may by law provide that neither the Supreme Court nor any other court shall exercise jurisdiction in respect of any such dispute or complaint as is referred to in Clause (1).

Entry 56 of List I of Seventh Schedule

Entry 56 of List I of Seventh Schedule provides that "Regulation and development of inter-State rivers and river valleys to the extent to which such regulation and development under the control of the Union is declared by Parliament by law to be expedient in the public interest."

Entry 17 under List II of Seventh Schedule

Entry 17 under List II of Seventh Schedule provides that "Water, that is to say, water supplies, irrigation and canals, drainage and embankments, water storage and water power subject to the provisions of Entry 56 of List I." As such, Central government is conferred with powers to regulate and develop inter-state rivers under Entry 56 of List I of Seventh Schedule to the extent declared by Parliament by the law to be expedient in the public interest. It also has the power to make laws for the adjudication of any dispute relating to waters of inter-state river or river valley under Article 262 of the Constitution.

The Karnataka is the eighth largest state in the country and is located in the Deccan plateau. The geographical area of Karnataka is 1,90,498 km^2

accounting for 5.81 per cent of the total area of the country. The climate of Karnataka varies from very humid rainy monsoon climate in the West Coast, the *Ghats* and *Malnad* areas to semiarid warm dry climate on the east. There is a large variation in the rainfall with higher amounts in the Western Ghats and reducing towards the eastern plains. Along the coastal Dakshina Kannada District, the normal rainfall is about 4,000 mm and in the drought-prone districts of Bijapur, Raichur, Bellary, etc., the rainfall is of the order of 500 mm to 600 mm. The average annual yield of the rivers of Karnataka has been roughly estimated as 98,406 m.cum (3475 tmc). The basin-wise breakup of this yield is given in Table 7.2.

Table 7.2

Basin-wise Average Annual Yield of the River of Karnataka

Sl. No.	*River System*	*Estimated Average Yield in*		
		m.cum	*tmc*	*Percentage*
1.	Krishna	27,451	969.44	27.90
2.	Kaveri	12,034	425.00	12.23
3.	Godavari	1,415	49.97	1.44
4.	West Flowing river	56,600	1998.83	57.51
5.	North Pennar	906	32.00	0.92
6.	South Pennar			
7.	Palar			
	Total	98406	3475.24	100

Source: Compiled from Annual Reports.

However, the economically utilisable water potential for irrigation is about 48,000 m.cum (1695 tmc). Agriculture being the main occupation of the state, irrigation plays utmost significant part in obtaining increased yields from the land. The development of irrigation in the state was slow and unsystematic during the pre-independence era. However, there were some notable irrigation works undertaken and completed during the pre-independence, such as Krishnaraja Sagar (which was the only major project completed prior to independence), Vijayanagar canals, Kaveri anicut Channels, Gokak Canal, Vanivilasa Sagar, Markonahalli and Anjanapura. Although major projects like Tungabhadra, Bhadra and Ghataprabha stage-I were commenced prior to the plan period, their progress was slow and they got impetus only after their inclusion in the first five year plan.

The Karnataka Irrigation Department, one of the major department in Government of Karnataka (GoK), is headed by the Hon'ble Minister for Major and Medium Irrigation. The Department harnesses surface water for irrigation and drinking water purposes.

The Department of Mines and Geology and Rural Engineering Department is responsible for the assessment and harness of groundwater resources for various purposes respectively. The construction, maintenance and monitoring of minor irrigation projects will come under the purview of minor irrigation department. The Karnataka Power Corporation Limited is responsible for generation of hydroelectric power. The Bangalore Water Supply and Sewerage Board are responsible for providing drinking water supply to Bangalore City. The Karnataka Urban Water Supply and Sewerage Board is responsible for providing drinking water supply to urban areas throughout the state of Karnataka.

The Karnataka Neeravari Nigam Limited (KNNL) was incorporated in 1998, under the company's act, as a wholly owned company of the GoK to expedite the completion of the ongoing irrigation projects in Krishna Valley. This is the second company in the state, the first being Krishna Bhagya Jala Nigam Limited (KBJNL), which was incorporated in 1994 to complete the Upper Krishna Project. The state government has transferred 10 projects to the KNNL for implementation, out of 28 major and medium irrigation projects in Krishna Basin. The Managing Director, KNNL, is incharge of this corporate body.

Water Resources in Karnataka

The average annual yield of the rivers of Karnataka has been roughly estimated as 98,406 m.cum. (3,475 tmc).

However, the economically utilisable water potential for irrigation is about 48,000 m.cum (1,695 tmc).

Basin-wise Master Plans

The state has prepared master plans for the various river basins. According to these plans, the total utilisation under major, medium and minor irrigation projects, using surface water, is 1,690.30 tmc (Table 7.3).

Table 7.3

Basin-wise Description

Sl.No.	*Particulars*	*Ultimate Utilisation (in tmc)*
• -	As per the Krishna Tribunal's (Krishna Water Disputes Tribunal) allocation presently in force	734.00
-	Available to the state, in Krishna Basin, by way of Godavari Diversion to Krishna, as per Godavari Ttibunal's (GWDT) award	23.00
-	Available to the state when the surplus waters of the Krishna river are allocated under scheme 'B' formulated by the Krishna Water Disputes Tribunal. This scheme can come into force on the formation of an authority to be called Krishna Valley Authority, either by consent of the party-states or by an act of Parliament	183.00
-	Available to the state when a section known as Peninsular Rivers Development (PRD) scheme materialises	216.00
	Total for Krishna Basin	**1156 .00**
•	Kaveri	408.62
•	Godavari	22.37
•	Other basins	103.31
	Total for the state	**1690.30**

Source: Compiled from Annual Reports.

Karnataka Neeravari Nigam Limited (KNNL)

KNNL is a state public sector undertaking incorporated on December 1998, with the prime objective of completing the irrigation projects in the Krishna river basin of Karnataka, excluding the upper Krishna Project being built by the KBJNL and other irrigation projects in Karnataka as allotted by GoK and has drawn its vision, mission and objectives indicating the targets to be achieved. The main objectives of KNNL are:

- Plan, investigate, design, estimate, build, operate and maintain irrigation projects in the Krishna river basin of Karnataka, excluding the Upper Krishna Project being built by the KBJNL.
- Prepare detailed project reports and estimates of such irrigation projects and build them after GoK obtains necessary approvals and sanctions the project administratively.
- Resettle and rehabilitate people affected by the building of irrigation projects.

Figure 7.1

River Basins of Karnataka

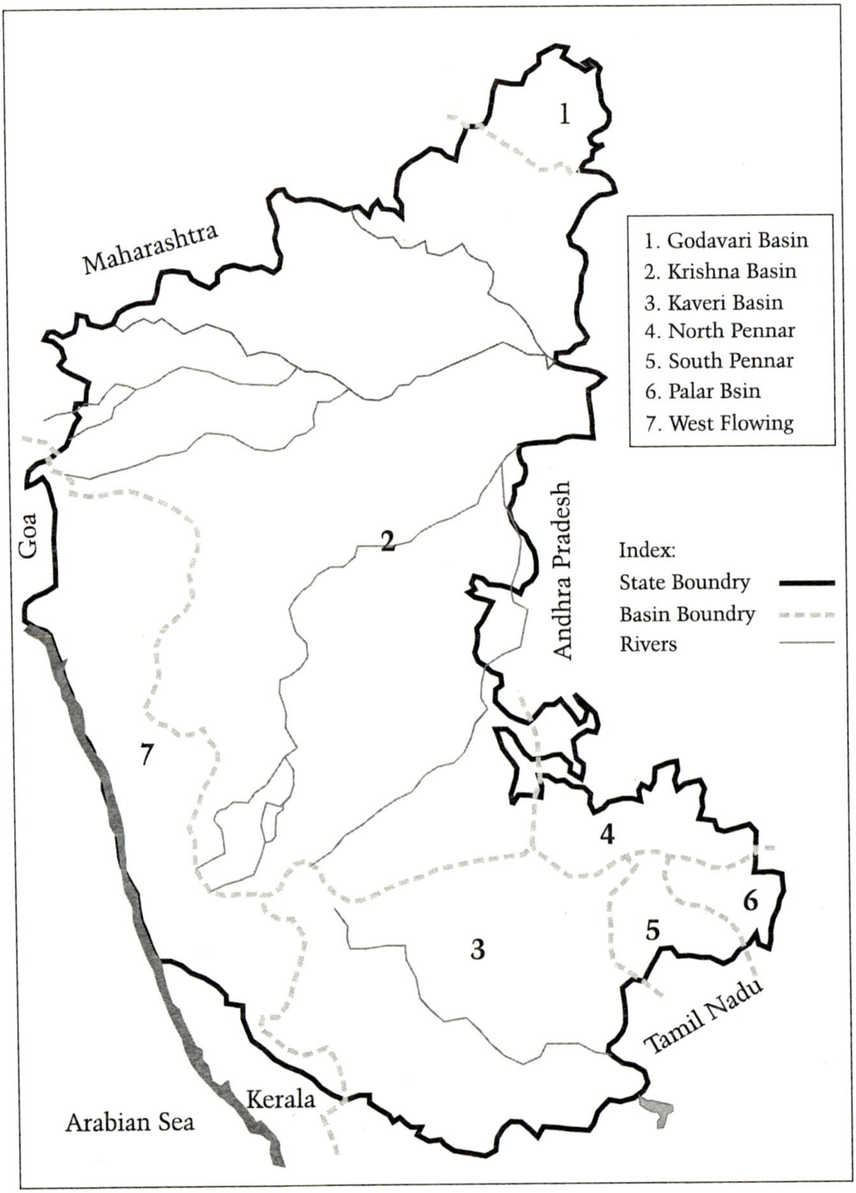

Source: Compiled from Annual Reports.

- Protect and improve the overall environment through appropriate measures, including treatment of the catchment areas of irrigation projects and afforestation.
- Adopt appropriate standards and specifications for the construction and maintenance of irrigation projects, draw up fresh standards/specifications, wherever necessary, and enforce modern quality assurance procedures.
- Promote schemes for flood control in the project areas.
- Promote schemes for navigation in the rivers where irrigation projects are being implemented and for leisure activities, fisheries, etc., in the water bodies of these projects.
- Promote adoption of modern irrigation methods like sprinkler, drip, etc., and the use of new materials and technologies in building irrigation projects.
- Promote schemes for utilising water from the irrigation projects built by the company.

KNNL has been registered as a wholly owned GoK company as per the provisions of the Companies Act, 1956, with effect from December 9, 1998. The Nigam aims at reviewing the planning and design aspects and monitoring the progress of the work and tracking field periodically by involving dedicated professional administrators, subject specialist and experienced engineers and other specialists in the field, in order to clear bottlenecks and ensure time bound progress of work.

All projects are required to meet the highest quality standards. The Nigam aims at initiating package contacts to ensure unit-wise completion of projects. A comprehensive approach is being followed by integration and synchronisation of all the components of the projects so that the main aim of providing water up to the field level can be achieved and the goal of utilisation of irrigation potential is realised.

The Nigam intends to give more thrust to new areas of development such as participatory irrigation management, encouragement to modern irrigation practices with more duty of water, exploration of new possibility of conjunctive use of water, advocating a holistic approach towards agricultural farming practices for economic security to the farmers and using modern technologies in survey and design of canal systems.

Management

The company is managed by the Board of Directors. Shri B.S. Yeddiyurappa, Chief Minister of Karnataka, is the Chairman of the board. The Managing Director of the company Shri D. Satya Murty, IAS, looks after the day-to-day affairs of the company. A team of professionally qualified and experienced personnels in various fields like civil and structural engineering, design, finance, project management, general administration and law assists the Managing Director. The Nigam aims at reviewing the planning and design aspects and monitoring the progress of the work and tracking field periodically by involving dedicated professional administrators, subject specialist and experienced engineers and other specialists in the field, in order to clear bottlenecks and ensure time bound progress of work.

Resources

The company's operations were entirely funded by GoK. The GoK provided ₹ 99.78 crore against the budgetary grant of ₹ 1,413.21 crore during 2008-09. The company has repaid the Series VI bonds amounting to ₹ 31.00 crore to bond holders who had exercised the option.

Quality Assurance

All projects are required to meet the highest quality standards. The Nigam aims at initiating package contacts to ensure unit-wise completion of projects. A comprehensive approach is being followed by integration and synchronisation of all the components of the projects, so that the main aim of providing water up to the field level can be achieved and the goal of utilisation of irrigation potential is realised.

A New Prospective

The Nigam intends to give more thrust to new areas of development such as participatory irrigation management, encouragement to modern irrigation practices with more duty of water, exploration of new possibility of conjunctive use of water, advocating a holistic approach towards agricultural farming practices for economic security to the farmer and using modern technologies in survey and design of canal systems.

Performance of KNNL

During the year 2009, KNNL is hanling about 44 irrigation projects, which include 26 ongoing projects, 11 projects to be started and 5 projects for modernisation. During 2009, GoK entrusted the Shiggon Li Scheme, estimated at a cost of ₹ 238 crore, which would provide irrigation to 9900 ha in the *talukas* of Shiggon, Savanur and Hanagal of Haveri districts. The total estimated cost of 33 projects under Krishna basin is ₹ 15,038 crore. During 2009, canal modernisation schemes of Bhadra, Tunga Bhadra, Vijayanagar channel, and Gondi Anicuts were undertaken. The details of the project that were undertaken are discussed. Table 7.4 depicts the status of projects that had to be completed by 2004-05. It is seen that some of the projects are still pending.

Ghataprabha Project

The project comprises a reservoir across the river Ghataprabha, near Hidkal in Hukkeri *taluka* to provide irrigation to 3,10,823 ha in Belgaum and Bagalkot districts. Potential created to the end of January 2007 is 2,90,928 ha.

Ghataprabha Right Bank Canal (GRBC)

Out of total length of 199.093 km, a length of 119 km, has been completed except lining works in 82, 83 and 92 km. Water has been let out for irrigation up to 119 km. Works are completed from 128 to 130, 132 to 136, 138 to 145, 147 to 186, 188 to 190, 195 and 196 km. In 120-121, 123-124 and 125-126 km, fresh agencies for the balance work have been fixed and the works are nearing to completion. In 135 km, agency stopped the work and contract has been rescinded and fresh tenders for balance work has been invited. In the remaining reaches works are under various stages of progress up to 199.093 km. There is a major aqueduct in 160 km and the work is completed.

Table 7.4

Performance of KNNL

SL No.	Projects	Latest Estimated Cost	Cumulative Expenditure up to 9/2001 since Inception	Balance Cost as on September 31, 2001	AWP for 2001-02	Expenditure during 2001-02 up to 9/2001	Proposed Year of Completion	Status as on March 31, 2009
1.	Ghataprabha	947.00	509.99	437.01	155.00	46.2	2003-04	Extended and on going
2.	Malaprabha	816.00	608.29	207.80	75.00	34.75	2002-03	Extended and on going
3.	Hippargi	901.00	52.08	848.92	25.00	7.32	2004-05	Bridge works completed. Third stage works are still in progress
4.	Markandeya	223.00	100.96	122.04	50.00	29.21	2002-05	Completed
5.	Harinala	42.00	32.75	9.25	17.00	1.77	2002-03	Completed
6.	U.T.P	915.35	148.11	767.24	100.00	53.93	2004-05	Completed
7.	Singatalur	595.00	23.77	571.23	35.00	3.18	2004-05	Work under progress
8.	Bhima Lift	187.58	8.85	178.73	10.00	1.50	2003-04	Work under progress
9.	Gandorinala	132.95	64.63	68.32	25.00	7.56	2003-04	Extended and on going
10.	Tunga Lift	24.12	0.00	24.12	2.00	-	2002-03	Works would be takenup
11.	Kalasa Nala	44.78	0.01	44.77	3.00	-	2002-03	Work in progress
	Total	4,877.98	1,549.46	3,328.52	500.00	185.42		

Source: Compiled from Annual Reports.

Distributaries

There are total 37 distributory blocks under GRBC. Works of distributory blocks 1 to 30 and block no. 33 are completed and works in distributory blocks 31, 32, 34, 35, 36 and 37 are under various stages of progress.

Branch Canal (CBC: 88 km)

The length of the canal is completed to its full length of km 88 and water let out for irrigation.

Distributories under CBC (25 nos.)

Works are completed in all blocks except block no. 21. The works of block no. 21 were held up due to forest clearance. The forest clearance is now received from Ministry of Environment and Forest (MoEF), GoI. Under block no. 21 (total length is 40 km), works completed up to 15 km and works were under progress from 16 km to 29 km.

Ghataprabha Left Bank Canal (GLBC): GLBC has been completed to its full length of 109 km and water has been let out for irrigation in all 61 blocks.

Malaprabha Project

Malaprabha Project comprises a dam across the river Malaprabha, near Navilutheertha in Belgaum district to provide irrigation to an extent of 2,20,028 ha in Belgaum, Bagalkot, Gadag and Dharwad districts. Potential created till the end of January 2007 is 2,03,541 ha.

- *Malaprabha Left Bank Canal (MLBC)*: Total length of MLBC is 150 km. The works are generally completed up to 150 km and water has been let out for irrigation up to 126 km.
- *Distributaries*: There are 58 distributory blocks under MLBC. Works of distributory blocks from 1 to 54 and 56A have been completed and works in distributory block no. 55 is under progress. Block 57 and 57(A) work are also under progress. The 58th block's tenders are finalised and works are under progress.

- *Malaprabha Right Bank Canal (MRBC)*: Total length of MRBC is 142 km. Work is completed up to 131 km. Water has been let out for irrigation up to 129.7 km. From 132 to 142 km, works are nearing completion except 137 km in which work is held up due to land acquistition problem.
- *Distributaries*: There are 60 distributory blocks under MRBC. Works of distributory blocks from 1 to 52 and block no. 54, 55B and 56A have been completed and works in distributory block no. 53A, 53(B) and 55A, 57 and 58 are under progress.

Hipparagi Project

Dam and Allied works

Barrage proper: The barrage works are completed.

Crest gates: Fabrication and erection of crest gates are completed and water is impounded (stored) in the reservoir.

Lifting systems: The works for the lifting systems of two foreshore lift irrigation schemes (LISs), namely, Halyal and Ainapur on turnkey basis are entrusted. The works of Ainapur lifting system and Halyal Stage-II are nearing completion and the works of Halyal Stage-I are under progress. Works of Karimasuthi III stage and Savalgi-Tungal IV Stage under Halyal LIS are under progress.

Canal works: The work of combined canal of Ainapur LIS and up to 9 km of Ainapur east canal, is under progress. Agencies fixed from 1 to 9 km of Ainapur west canal, from 1 to 5 km and 11 to 35 km of Halyal east canal, from 1 to 10 km of Halyal west canal and from 0 to 7.42 km of Savalagi-Tungal west canal and works are under progress. Tenders opened for Ainapur east canal from 10 to 20 km and same is under process for approval. Tenders are invited from 36 to 40 km of Halyal east canal, from 0 to 10 km of Savalgi-Tungal, from 0 to 10 km of Karimasuthi east canal including combined canal of Karimasuthi LIS. In the balance reaches under Ainapur & Halyal LIS survey works, approval to general alignment, design and preparation of estimates are under progress. Survey works, preparation of general alignment of Karimasuthi and Savalgi-Tungal east and west canal are under progress.

Markandeya Project

Dam and Allied works: The dam and allied works have been entrusted to Kerala State Construction Corporation (KSCC) Ltd. The conncreting work of dam is completed, dyke works are also completed. Construction of parapet is under progress. The fabrication and erection of six crest gates are completed.

Canal works: Total length of Markandeya Left Bank Canal is 15 km, works in 7 to 15 km are completed. Works are under progress from 1 to 6 km. The right bank canal (RBC) has a length of 71 km. Works are almost completed from 1 to 71 km. Water is let out on trial run basis up to 65 km.

Distributories: Total numbers of distributory blocks are 45. Works in block no. 1 to 11 and 14 to 45 are completed. Works in other blocks are under progress.

Harinala Project

Harinala project envisages construction of an earthen dam across Harinala, a tributary to river Malaprabha to irrigate 3,480 ha in Bailahongal *taluka* of Belgaum district.

Dam and Allied works: The dam works including head regulators for left bank canal (LBC) and RBC are completed. Water is impounded in the dam.

Canal works: The entire length of RBC (11 km) and LBC (9 km) is completed. Total potential of 3,480 ha under this project has been created. Fabrication and installation works completed.

R&R (Reclamation and Rehabilitation) works: The project involves partial submergence of only one village involving 58 families. R&R works are completed.

Upper Tunga Project

Upper Tunga Project envisages construction of a new dam 100 m downstream of the existing Tunga anicut near Gajanur in Shimoga district to irrigate 80,494 ha in Shimoga, Honnali, Haveri, Harihara, Hirekerur, Ranebennur and Hanagal *talukas*.

Project Comprises:

Dam

Canal: 329.5 km.

Distributory network for 80,494 ha.

Dam and Allied works: Dam work including parapet wearing coat and asphalting works is completed and preparation of final bill is under progress. All the 22 gates are erected. Electrification work is completed. Work of drawing of 11 KVA powerline for power connection work is completed and inspection from inspectorate is completed. The instrumentation work is completed. Power block portion of mini hydel project is completed and further work of power house is to be taken up by private agency. Agreement for lease of land to that agency is executed. Earthwork excavation for construction of power house and tail race channel has started

Bhima Lift Project

Bhima Lift Irrigation Scheme comprises a barrage near Sonna village of Afzalpur *taluka* in Gulbarga district to irrigate 24,292 ha in Gulbarga district through two foreshore lift points. Original estimated cost (based on SR of 1993-94) is ₹ 107.70 crore. Revised estimate cost (based on SR of 2004-05) is ₹ 275.53 crore.

Doodhganga Project

Doodhganga Irrigation Project is an inter-state project of Maharastra and Karnataka. The project envisages construction of composite dam across the river Doodhganga near village Asangaon of Radhanagari *taluka* in Kolhapur District of Maharastra. This project would provide irrigation benefits to 46,948 ha in Maharastra and 15,167 ha in Karnataka. The planned utilisation is 27.43 tmc. Potential created till the end of January 2007 is 3800 ha. The original estimated cost is ₹ 124.00 crore (based on SR of 1999-2000).

Allocation for Karnataka State: 4.00 tmc

Project comprises from first entry into Karnataka.

25.607 km long Nidhori branch canal (as per project report length = 23.607 km; as per actual report length = 25.607 km).

21.875 km long Bidri branch canal as per actual (as per project report length = 48.36 km).

9 km long Kurundawad branch canal.

27.70 km long Dattawad branch canal (after entering into Karnataka border) with their distribution system.

Gandorinala Project

Dam and allied works: The works were carried out by KSCC and the same are already completed. The work of providing and erection of radial crest gates is completed.

Canal works: RBC: Completed to its full length of 7 km.

LBC: Total length of LBC is 90 km. The works are completed from 0 to 23 km, 24 to 25 km nearing completion and 25 to 36 km under progress. From 36 to 60 km, work has completed, except for 500 m for which there is land acquisition problem. Work from 61 to 90 km is under progress.

Distributories: Under RBC, distributory works have been completed in all three blocks and under LBC 18 blocks are completed. 17 block works are under progress. Work for 4 blocks to be started.

FIC: From 0 to 7 km of RBC and from 0 to 20 km of LBC, works are nearing completion. FIC from 20 to 60 km works are under progress and from 61 to 90 km, survey work is under progress.

Lower Mullamari Project

The Lower Mullamari Project is a medium irrigation project, across river Mullamari, a tributary to river Kagina in Bheema sub-basin. The Project is located near Nagaral village in Chincholi *taluka*, Gulbarga District to provide irrigation facility to 8,100 ha of land in Chincholi *taluka* of Gulbarga District.

Project Comprises: (a) earthen dam: work completed including erection of spillway gates. Water is being stored in reservoir from August 2001; (b) RBC: works are completed (80 km); (c) laterals (11 nos): 6 in progress, 5 are completed; (d) distributaries (66 nos): 64 are completed. Lining work is in progress for 2 distributories and is nearing completion.

Bennithora Project

The Bennithora Irrigation Project is a major irrigation project across Bennithora river, a major tributary of river Kagina in Bheema sub-basin. The project is located near village Herur (K) in Chittapur *taluka* of Gulbarga District to provide irrigation facility to 20,234 ha of land in Chitapur and Sedam *taluka* of Gulbarga Dist.

Earthen Dam: Work is completed and water is being stored in reservoir, since August 2001.

Right Bank Canal (82 km): Works are completed.

Sub-distributories on major distributory (12 nos.): 10 completed, 2 in progress.

Distributaries under RBC (40 nos): 38 are completed, 2 in progress.

Laterals for sub-distributory (8 nos.): 8 under progress.

DPO (36 Nos.): 34 completed, 2 in progress.

LBC (60 km): Works are completed.

Gtalur Lift Irrigation Scheme

The project comprises of construction of a barrage across Tungabhadra river near Hammige village of Mundargi *taluka* in Gadag district, to provide an irrigation facilities to an extent of 1,20,236 acres (1,40,677acres of cropped area) with the irrigation intensity of 117 per cent using 12.03 tmc of water as per the directions of the KNNL board during the 24 the meeting held on February 22, 2005. The Board noted that the economic viability of the scheme would improve with the modification and approve the physical cropped area, Stage-I with an utilisation of 7.64 tmc to irrigate 76,181 acre and Stage-II with an utilisation of 4.39 tmc to irrigate 44,055 acre. Accordingly the Chief Engineer, Irrigation Central Zone, Munirabad, submitted the modified detail project report and revised estimate costing ₹ 657.00 crore to this office for accordingly revised administrative approval. The same is submitted to Government for revised administrative approval vide letter no. 252 dated April 21, 2005. Government has accorded administrative approval to implement this scheme with the utilisation of 12.03 tmc of water in the GO dated June 29, 2006. The works of preparation of EIA/EMP reports, in respect of SLIS, is entrusted to Bangalore University and reports have been submitted.

Barrage: The GoK has directed to continue the balance works of Barrage and other allied works through M/s. KSCC vide Government Order (GO) dated December 6, 2003. Accordingly, the works are taken up. Out of 26 blocks concreting in all the blocks has reached up to crest level except in block no. 6 and 7. The entire spillway blocks have reached the crest level except block no. 6 and 7. Pier concreting is under progress. Concreting in power block is in progress. Concerting of non-overflow section on right side is under progress. The work of protection bund on left side is in progress. Fabrication of gates is completed. Barrage work started after recedance of flood

Tunga Lift Project

The works in respect of these projects have not commenced for want of forest clearance. Proposal requesting permission for survey/diversion of wild life sanctuary etc., is submitted to State Forest Department for onward submission to GoI. Principal Chief Conservator of Forest (PCCF) has sought opinion of PCCF (West Lift [WL]). It is learnt that PCCF has obtained the opinion of PCCF (WL) and has submitted his opinion on the matter to Principal Secretary of Forest Ecology and Environment Department (FEE), recently. Further, action from Principal Secretary is awaited.

Kalasanala and Bandurnala Projects

These two projects envisage diversion of 7.56 tmc of water to Malaprabha dam by constructing dam across the above *nalas* and diversion canals.

Administrative approval for these two projects was accorded by Government in August 2000.

Proposal for diversion of about 500 ha. submitted to MoEF, GoI, by state government.

The presentation has already been made in forest advisory committee meeting. Forest clearance is pending for want of Central Water Commission (CWC) clearance for the project. The formal clearance given by the CWC has been kept under abeyance.

Estimate and DTP for Kalasa dam works are finalised.

Estimate and DTP for Bandur Nala are under finalisation.

The KNNL board has recommnended in its 25th meeting held on June 7, 2005, to take up the works in non-forest area by entrusting the work to any government firm. Accordingly a letter has been addressed to government vide this office letter no. KNN/MP/Mahadayi/88/2003-04999 dated June 23, 2005. Government has ordered to take up the works in non-forest area under Kalasa and Banduranala projects vide GO dated October 9, 2006. Work has started in Kalasanala project in non-forest area on October 13, 2006.

Itagi Sasalwad Project

The project envisages lifting of 1.540 cumecs of water from left bank of Tungabhadra river near Itagi village to irrigate 1,983.80 ha of lands coming in 12 villages of Shirahatti and Mundaragi *taluka* in Gadag District and Haveri *taluka* in Haveri District.

Basapur Project

The Project envisages of lifting 1.60 cumecs of water from Varada river and to irrigate 2,266 ha in Haveri District. The scheme comprises of 2 stages and irrigates 1,133 ha in each stage. Presently, first stage works are under progress.

Varahi Project

Varahi river is a major west flowing river in west coast. The river takes its origin near Guddakoppa village in Hosanagar *taluka*, Shimoga District. Across this river, a dam is constructed by KPCL near Mani village for power generation, there is a continuous tail race discharge of about 1,100 cumecs thoughout the year. It is proposed to make use of this water by constructing a diversion weir as major irrigation project. It is proposed to provide irrigation to 15,702 ha (flow: 12,979 ha and lift: 2,723 ha) in Udupi district.

Amarja Project

Amarja project is situated in Aland *taluka* of Gulbarga district. It envisages to provide irrigation to an extent of 8,903 ha in Aland and Afzalpur *talukas*.

Amarja Dam: Works are completed and water is being stored, since 1999.

The work is transferred to KNNL during April 2005 vide GO no. WRD/29/TMZ/04 dated April 18, 2005.

Javaluhalla LIS

The LIS from Javaluhalla near Kittur village of Ramdurga is proposed to feed suffering *atchkat* of 4,736 acres (1917 ha), under Sirasangi Dy. under National Building Code (NBC) of Malaprabha Right Bank Canal (MRBC). The head works, a *bhandara* of this scheme are located near Kittur village.

The LIS is entrusted on tender basis to M/s. Coramandel Prestcret Pvt. Ltd. Construction of *bhandara* pitching work is under progress. Construction of intake channel lining work is under progress. Construction of jackwell/pumphouse work finishing work is under progress. Construction of delivery chamber work is completed. Laying of 2100 m pipelines as a part of the main construction work was completed

Kolachi, Konnur and Bennihalla LIS

Kolachi LIS: The LIS is being constructed in Ron *taluka*, Gadag District. The scheme proposes to lift 2.59 cumecs of water per year at Asoti from Bennihalla for providing irrigation to suffering *atchkat* of 1,538 ha under KRBC.

Konnur LIS: It is constructed near Nargund *taluka* Gadag District. The scheme proposes to lift 0.39 tmc of water at Konnur from Malaprabha river for providing irrigation benefit to suffering *atchkat* of 1,587 ha under NBC. Work order issued to agency.

Bennihalla LIS: It is constructed near Nargund *taluka* Gadag District. The scheme proposes series of weirs at Banahatti, Kuralageri, Surkod, Khanapur and Raddeernagnur to irrigate the suffering *atchkat* of 3,868 ha under NBC. Work order is issued to agency and survey is under progress. The above LISs are entrusted to M/s SPML on turnkey basis. Actual site location survey by the agency has been completed. Land acquisition 4(1) notification is published. Power supply charges of ₹ 1,750 is remitted to Hubli Electricity Supply Company Ltd. (HESCOM).

5,770 mts of 600 mm dia is supplied at Khanapur LIS and 4,065 mts of 1,000 mm dia is supplied at Surkod LIS and 162 nos. of 1,000 mm dia is supplied at Khanapur LIS. Laying work is completed at Khanapur LIS i.e., 5,000 mtrs and 3,449 mtrs at Surkod LIS. Radder Naganur LIS-3210 mts of 600 mm dia is supplied and 850 mts laying work is completed. In Konnur LIS, 1485 mts dia is supplied, in Kolachi LIS, 790 mts of 1,000 dia is supplied and 380 mts laying work is completed.

Alignment of 5 location and pipe design are approved. Design and drawing for jackwell cum pumphouse and intake weir are approved, except Banahatti and Kurlageri LIS. Excavation for jack well at Radder-Naganur and Khanapur and Kolachi LIS completed.

Sri Mallapura LIS

The scheme envisages lifting 1.00 tmc of water in two stages from Varada river near Byatanal to irrigate 13,000 acres (5,261 ha) of lands in Byadagi *taluka* of Haveri District.

The above LIS is entrusted to M/s. Coramandel Prestcrete Pvt. Ltd., on turnkey basis.

Jackwell cum Pump house: Excavation completed and work is stopped due to flood in river.

Raising Main-I: Excavation for 3.5 km completed, out of 5.1 km. Manufacturing of pipes is, yet, to be commenced by the agency.

Delivery Chamber-I: Work is completed in all respect.

Gravity Canal-I: Excavation is completed. Out of 26 CD works, 4 CD works are completed and 12 CD works are under progress.

U.G. Sump and Pump house: U.G. sump is completed. Pump house columns and walls raised up to roof level.

Raising Main-II: Excavation is completed, 100 pipes arrived at the site, out of 200 pipes manufactured, and balances are to be manufactured.

Delivery Chamber-II: Work is completed in all respect.

Gravity Canal-II (Sudambi Canal): Excavation for 3.00 km is completed, out of 6.5 km.

Gravity Canal-III (Kaginele Canal): Excavation for 1.5 km is completed under progress, out of 14.50 km.

Pumps: Design and drawings of pumps for first and second stage are approved.

Motors: Design and drawing of motors for first and second stage were submitted to LIS consultant of Nigam and returned with observations, which are to complied.

Progress: Overall financial progress achieved till the end of January 2007 is ₹ 1,253.82 lakh.

Sri Rameshwara LIS

Sri Rameshwara LIS : This lift irrigation is proposed to irrigate 13,800 ha areas of Gokak, Ramadurga and Savadatti *talukas* of Belgaum District, by utilising the 2.2 tmc of water. The water will be drawn from Ghataprabha river by suitable intake structure. From jack well, water will be pumped to the extent of head 157.00 mtr (including losses), through the rising main of 2.20 m dia, which is of 17.50 km in length. Water shall be distributed through canal system from intermediate delivery chamber at RL 640.00 and delivery chamber at RL 660.00.

Excavation for the pumphouse and rising main for the length of 8 km is completed and further work is under progress.

Rising main pipes are manufactured as detailed below:

12 mm Thick 2.20 m dia: 1000.00 nos. i.e., 6000.00 mts.

8 mm Thick 1.50 m dia: 75.00 nos. i.e., 450.00 mts.

Pipes with inner coating 2.20 m dia: 400.00 nos. i.e., 2400.00 mts.

Pipes with outer coating 2.20 m dia: 380.00 nos. i.e., 2280.00 mts.

Land Acquistition: Intake channel, pump house, jack well and sub-station are located near Aralimatti Village covering an area of 5.10 acres for which 4(1) Notification has been issued and JMC is also completed.

Rising Main: Total length of rising main is 17.50 km. The alignment is passing through Aralimatti, Venkatapura, Kulgod, Koujalagi, Kalliguddi and Mannikeri villages covering an area of 51.00 acres. 4(1) Notification is issued and JMC is under progress.

Electro-mechanical Components: Finalisation of designs for electro mechanical equipments such as pumps, motors, EOT, switch gear panels, HT and LT capacitors, cubicles, temperature scanners, cabling and earthling system, 110 KV sub-station, valves, delivery and manifold pipe air chamber and air compressor, one way serge tank are completed.

Canal Network: Approximate length of main canal system is 69 km and approximate length of distribution system is 91 km. The detailed survey work and fixing of alignment, preparation of estimate and DTPs are to be taken up for which the decision from Nigam has already been taken up to entrust on tender basis by calling open tenders. The estimate for out-sourcing as above has been sanctioned for 85.16 lakh. A tender for the survey work is under evaluation stage. The work is yet to be awarded to the agency. This survey work including preparation of designs, estimates and DTPs is scheduled to complete within 4 months from the date of agreement.

Environmental Impact Assessment/Environmental Management Plan (EIA/EMP) Studies: This has been entrusted to Prof & Chairman, Department of Environment Sciences, Bangalore University, Bangalore, and report are yet to be received for the same.

Bellary Nala LIS

The Bellary nala irrigation project envisages to irrigate 8,200 ha of land in Gokak and Saudatti *talukas* of Belgaum District by constructing a dam across Bellary nala, which is a main tributory to Markendaya river.

The master plan committee has allocated 1.68 tmc of water under scheme 'A' of Krishna Water Dispute Tribunal (KWDT).

The work construction of Bellary nala irrigation project has been entrusted to M/s EPI Ltd. (a GoI undertaking) by GoI.

The excavation for dam foundation is under progress.

Concreting in block no. 1 to 6 and 10 to 18 is under progress.

Survey for canal network is under progress.

Hiranyakeshi LIS

Under Hiranyakeshi LIS, it is proposed to lift 8 tmc of water from Hiranyakeshi river to feed GRBC during *khariff* season.

8.00 tmc of water has been allocated under scheme 'A' of KWDT.

This scheme has been proposed to meet the likely shortage of water, due to over utilisation under GLBC.

The said LIS has been entrusted to M/s Kirloskar Brothers Pvt. Ltd., on turnkey basis.

The intake channel work is under progress.

The alignment of jack well and raising is approved.

Amruthapura-Ubrani LIS

The Ubrani-Amruthapura LIS envisages to stabilise 11,818 acres of land in Chennagiri and Tarikere *taluka* by lifting of water from upstream of a diversion structure across Bhadra river near Kodinahalli village near Bhadravathi.

The master plan committee has allocated 1.25 tmc of water under scheme 'A' of KWDT.

The head works first stage is entrusted to M/s SPML.

The works of intake channel is in progress.

Raising main work is in progress.

Physical Performance

During the year, GoK has entrusted to the company the Shiggon LIS at an estimated cost of ₹ 238 crore for providng irrigation to 9900 Ha in the *talukas* of Shiggon, Savanur and Hanagal of Haveri Districts and also to fill the existing MI tanks and Bandaras within the command of the proposed project for drinking purpose. Besides the Dandavathi Medium Irrigation project in Shikaripura *taluka* of Shimoga District was also entrusted during the year. The GoI had approved ₹ 1435 crore as revised cost for Ghataprabha and ₹ 1275 crore to Malaprabha project. The central assistance under AIBP based on the revised costs estimated of ₹ 592 crore has been granted. The revised cost of Gandorinala Project is ₹ 240 crore, which was approved by the GoI. Tables 7.5 and 7.6 depicts the physical efficiency of projects that were undertaken and the time and cost overrun.

Table 7.5

Project-wise Cost Overrun

Projects	*Original cost of the project*	*Revised cost*	*Cost overrun*
Ghataprabha	947.00	1435	488
Malaprabha	816.00	1275	459
Bhima Lift	187.58	592	405
Gandorinala	132.95	240	108

Source: Compiled from Annual Reports.

Table 7.6

Project-wise Time Overrun

Projects	*Proposed Year of Completion*	*Status (as on March 31, 2009)*	*Time Overrun (yrs)*
Ghataprabha	2003-04	2008-09	5
Malaprabha	2002-03	2008-09	6
Hippargi	2004-05	2008-09	4
Singatalur	2004-05	2008-09	4
Bhima Lift	2003-04	2008-09	5
Gandorinala	2003-04	2008-09	5
Tunga Lift	2002-03	2008-09	7
Kalasa Nala	2002-03	2008-09	7

Source: Compiled from Annual Reports.

Table 7.6 depicts the time overrun of 6-7 years for various projects to complete all the originally started projects. This led to a considerable amount on revenue expenditure of the company, which was unpredicted, and also finding a source for acquiring the funds may be difficult, in view of global financial scenario.

Financial Performance

Resource Mobilistion

The company operations were entirely funded by the GoK. The GoK provided ₹ 991.78 crore against the budgetary grant of ₹ 1,413 crore during fiscal year (FY) 2008-09. The company paid ₹ 31.00 crore, worth of Series IV bonds to the bond holders. The GoK has provided a budgetary support of ₹ 1,943.04 crore including debt servicing for the company for 2009-10.

Loans and Advances

The company had issues non-convertible redeemable bonds of ₹ 257 crore during 2009. The term loan from Oriental Bank of Commerce, which is repayable in two equal installments on March 31, 2011, and 2012, amounted to ₹ 100 crore. The other term loan from Bank of Baroda, repayable in two equal installments on March 31, 2011, and March 31, 2012, amounted to ₹ 199 crore. The third term loan from Dena Bank, repayable in two equal installments on March 31, 2012 and 2013, amounted to ₹ 50 crore.

Table 7.7

Loans and Advances

Year	*Bonds*	*Term Loan*	*Total Loan*
2004-05	969.00	1189	2158.00
2005-06	784.00	1194	1978.00
2006-07	516.00	350	866.00
2007-08	288.00	350	638.00
2008-09	257.00	350	607.00

Source: Compiled from Annual Reports.

Figure 7.2

Loans and Advances

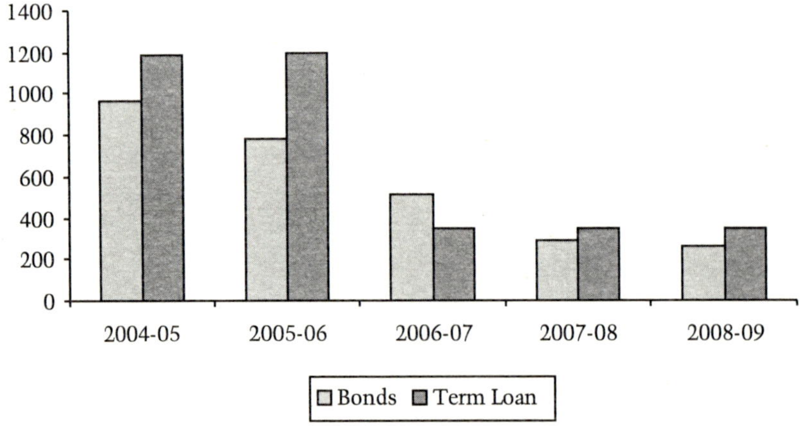

Source: Compiled from Annual Reports.

Current Assets to Current Liabilities

The current ratio is a measure of the corporate short-term solvency. It indicates the availability of current assets in rupees for every one rupee of current liability. A ratio greater than one means that the corporation has more current assets. The company is generating significant results with respect to this ratio:

Table 7.8

Current Ratio

Year	*CA*	*CL*	*Current Ratio*
2004-05	399.00	161.00	2.48
2005-06	474.00	176.00	2.69
2006-07	613.00	200.00	3.07
2007-08	278.00	373.00	0.75
2008-09	479.00	465.00	1.03

Note: CA: current asset; CL: current liability.

Figure 7.3

Current Ratio

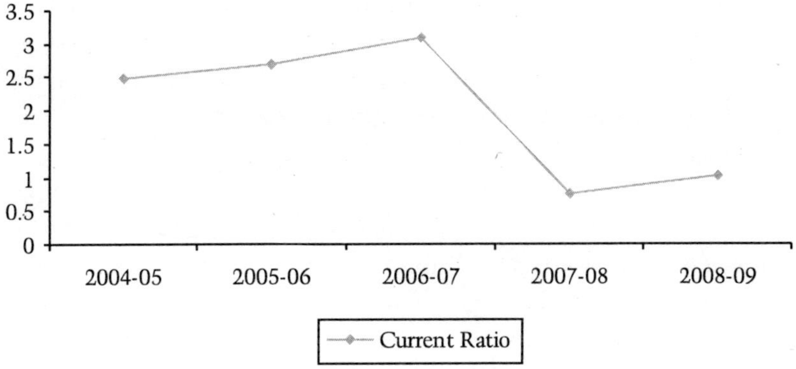

The company has incurred expenditure towards payment of interest on borrowed funds. Since, all the projects that were originally scheduled to be completed by the 2003-04 and 2004-05 could not be completed; hence, there is a cost overrun for the four projects that stood at ₹ 1,406 crore.

This also became another burden on the companies finances. In view of the above, it is suggested that either the company can acquire low-cost funds/ bonds or the GoK may give support to the company.

Corporate Social Responsibility

As a part of the modernisation to the irrigation management and to bring in the farmers involvement, the KNNL has adopted the participatory irrigation management under the corporate social responsibility (CSR) scheme. As a part of the CSR initiative, the members of the Water Users' Society (WUS) were involved in distributing the water resources. This consists of not less than 60 per cent of the water users for cultivation of land. Though the WUS have been entrusted with several functions, the main function is to procure water in bulk on volumetric basis from the KNNL and distribute it to the land holders in accordance with the principles laid down by the General Body for equitable distribution of water. In addition to these functions, they can also operate and maintain canal within their jurisdiction. Other main function of the society include: (i) to levy and collect water charges and services charges from the land holders; (ii) to develop irrigation infrastructure by availing institutional finance; (iii) to procure water in bulk on volumetric basis from the Irrigation Department or KBJNL or KNNL and distribute it to the land holders in accordance with the principles laid down by the General Body for equitable distribution of water; (iv) to operate and maintain canals situated within its jurisdiction; (v) to levy and collect water charges and service charges from the land holders; (vi) to educate and train land holders in the efficient and economical use of water and adoption of new technology as well as to implement necessary programmes; (vii) to prepare water budget and financial budget for each irrigation season; (viii) to resolve disputes that may arise among land holders; (ix) to mobilise financial resources for undertaking activities and efficient management of the society.

The benefits of modernisation would increase production with capital cost increase and decrease in O&M cost again, resulting in efficiency, equity, design complexity and least operation staff requirements. The company has completed Harinala (3,480 ha) and Markandeya (19,105 ha) projects in record time and is able to release the water to the fields of farmers. The company is experiencing smiles on the face of farmers in the drought-prone areas of northern Karnataka. Further, the company is able to complete the Bennithora project and Lower Mullamari Projects within three years of transfer to the company, which were lingering for the last 30 years.

The company before implementing the project has to obtain environmental & forest clearances from the MoEF for clearances both from GoK & GoI based on research studies by the qualified professionals including NEERI (National Environment & Ecological Research Institute). The company also agrees for compensation, if any, including afforestation and catchment area treatment plan for the above, if affected on the construction of the projects as per the Department claims.

The company has also contributed ₹ 5.00 lakh toward CM Relief Fund under CSR scheme.

Memorandum of Understanding (MoU)

The Department of Public Enterprise and KNNL has entered into MoU for an effective evaluation and monitoring of the performance of the KNNL. The main mission for entering the MoU is as follows:

- To execute the projects as directed by the government under the guidance and advice of the board.
- To ensure completion of the projects in speedy way, subject to the availability of funds.

As a part of MoU, full financial support is essential by way of grants under the budgetary support for capital expenditure and establishment, and other revenue expenditures for the year 2009-10 amounts to ₹ 1878 crore.

SWOT Analysis

The key strengths, weaknesses, opportunities and threats (SWOT) of KNNL are presented below:

Strengths

- High source of water for construction of irrigation projects.
- It reduces the work load and time required for agriculture.

- Improved quantity and timeliness of water supply to crops.
- Reduces damage from floods.
- Increases the production of crops.
- Reduces the poverty of families depend on agriculture.
- Indirectly helps to control the inflation.

Weaknesses

- Land acquisition for projects.
- Cost of construction of project is very high.
- Limited participation of farmers in project design, implementation and completion.
- Mostly depend on government guarantees for mobilisation of funds.
- No corporate plan to assess the requirement of funds.
- No periodical estimation of estimated projects and cost overrun.
- The progress of implementation of project is poor.
- No maintenance of database of ongoing projects.
- No proper survey and estimation prior to commencement of the work.
- Low collection of water charges and high administrative/ establishment expenditure.

Threats

- Legal problems from the farmers from whom land is acquired.
- Poor understanding of sustainable irrigation practices may lead to future environment problems.
- Political turmoil and change in the government policy.
- Increase in the cost of material or logistics.

Opportunities

- To increase the cultivated lands.
- Management of land for more production.

- New agricultural crops can be developed with eco-tourism.
- Improvement in cultivation, even by small farmers.

Conclusion and Recommendations

This chapter summarises the conclusion of the present study. It also enumerates the outlines and suggestions/recommendations based on evaluations and analysis:

- Corporate plan to assess the requirements of funds on long-term basis.
- The company can explore new financing instruments so as to reduce the debt component in the company to avail the leverage benefit.
- The Nigam intends to give more thrust to new areas of development such as participatory irrigation management, encouragement to modern irrigation practices with more duty of water, exploration of new possibility of conjunctive use of water, advocating a holistic approach towards agricultural farming practices for economic security to the farmer and using modern technologies in survey and design of canal systems.
- As the projects could not be completed in time, it is recommended that care must be taken to timely complete all the projects.
- The objectives of the company are framed well, which would address the basic needs of the human kind. Hence, GoK may take a strong view of financing the company in order to complete all the pending projects at the earliest, without incurring much more expenditure in the form of capital and revenue expenditure.
- It is observed that there is a time overrun of six to seven years to complete all the originally started projects. This led to a considerable amount on revenue expenditure of the company, which was unpredicted, and also finding a source for acquiring the funds might be also difficult in view of global financial scenario. The reason for not completing the projects on schedule is unknown. Hence, it is suggested to make an analysis in order,

not to repeat in future, as a controlling measure for effective utilisation of all the resources.

- Steps to increase internal generation of resources for projects.
- Minimise the administrative/establishment expenditure.
- Analysis has to be made in respect of problems, which led to considerable extra fund implication and time overrun.
- Steps to improve the collection of water charges.
- Periodical updating of the estimated projects with economical viability.
- Proper survey and estimation of the cost prior to commence of the projects.
- Maintenance of database showing the details of ongoing projects to improve the efficiency.

8 Horticultural Producers Cooperative Marketing and Processing Society

V. Srikanth

Background

Horticultural Producers Cooperative Marketing and Processing society Limited (HOPCOMS) was registered by the Registrar of Cooperative Societies vide registration No. 1827, dated September 10, 1959. The registered office of the society is located at Lalbagh, Bangalore, 560004. In January 2009, the Government of Karnataka (GoK) has declared it as the unit of Horticulture Department. The areas of operation of HOPCOMS are Bangalore urban, Bangalore rural, Kolar, Chikkaballapura and Ramanagar Districts. As per GoK order 2007, HOPCOMS has handed over the branches at Mysore, Mandya, Mangalore, Hassan and Chikkamagalur District to the respective district horticultural societies.

Management (Board Committee)

HOPCOMS, Bangalore, is being run under the agency and as a unit of Department of Horticulture. The Board of Management consists of 20 members; 11 members are elected from among the producers, and a few are GoK nominees. The Managing Director is an officer of the Horticulture Department on a lent service (deputation). The main objectives of this society is to promote and encourage development of horticultural produces. The other objectives are as follows:

- To train and provide technical advice and literature on horticultural crops.
- To provide inputs implements on plans and grafts etc.

- Providing cold storage facilities marketing facilities and also organising proper studies to the members of the society.
- To supply horticultural produces to all major factories, Government hospitals, Hostels, Clubs, and social functions like marriage, etc.
- Providing internal Commodities Exchange facilities to co-operative societies and branches.

Area of Operation

The present area of operation of HOPCOMS is extended to Bangalore urban, Bangalore rural d Kolar District, Chikkaballapur, Channaptna and Ramanthapur.

Membership

The membership of the society shall consist of:

- 'A' Class members: These are the individual horticultural producers residing in the area of operation of the society.
- 'B' class members: Associate members included in cooperative societies and other institutions.
- 'C' class members: State Government.
- Total share capital of HOPCOMS as on March 31, 2009, is ₹ 264.38 lakh. Details are shown below:

Share Capital

'A' class membership	-	₹ 16,268-30.67 lakh
'B' class membership	-	₹ 526-5.62 lakh
'C' class membership	-	₹ 228.09 lakh

Activities

At present the society is handling about 110 Mt of fruits and vegetables issued—about 75 per cent through retail outlets and 25 per cent to the institutions, vegetables daily. Nearly 195-200 farmers are daily bringing their produces directly to the society. As soon as the produces are received from the farmers, the produces in graded. Weighed and cash payment is made immediately.

The daily handling quantity details are:

- Bangalore: 100 MT.
- Kolar: 10 MT.
- Total: 110 MT.

Facilities Extended to the Farmers

HOPCOMS is offering multifarious facilities to the farmers:

- HOPCOMS purchases the horticulture produces directly from the farmers at remunerative prices.
- Provides transport facilities from collection centres.
- Provides weighment and immediate cash payment.
- Arranges input supply at reasonable prices.
- Arranges subsidised supply of plastic carters to its farmers, members to handle fruits and vegetables.
- Supplies seeds under subsidised rates.
- Assisting farmers towards technical guidance.
- Provides training on production and processing of horticultural crops.
- Provides accommodations for night stay.
- Provides canteen and banking facilities.
- Provides minimum support price (MSP) during distress sales under government schemes.

HOPCOMS staff details (as on 2008-09): At present HOPCOMS has 916 staff of different grades.

Table 8.1

Staff Details of HOPCOM, 2008-09

S.No	Particulars	No. of Staff
1.	Government officials (on Deputation)	04 MD, GM P&M Manager (A)
2.	Asst. Executive Engineers	1
3.	Managers	5
4.	Asst. Managers	5
5.	Superintendent	1
6.	FDA	27
7.	SDA	167
8.	Steno	1
9.	Senior Typist	7
10.	Assistants	679
11.	Drivers	18
12.	Security	01
	Total	916

Source: Compiled from Annual Reports.

Assets

Marketing of fruits and vegetables of the society consists the following facilities:

- Retail outlets: 318 (Bangalore: 279, Kolar: 39)
- Chemical and fertiliser outlet: 2
- Cold storages: 1 (Bangalore)
- Vehicles: 25 (Bangalore-23, Kolar-2)
- Processing unit: 1 (Bangalore)
- Walk in colors: 2 (Bangalore, Kolar)
- Grading unit: 1 (Bangalore)
- Procurement centers: 6 (Saljapur, Chanhiapattafla, Hosakote, Kanakapura Doddaballapur, & Malur)

Table 8.2

Immovable Assets

S.No.	Particulars	Assets Value (in lakh)
1.	Buildings	458.84
2.	Furniture	117.42
3.	Vehicles and machineries	192.92
	Total	769.20
1.	Investments and fixed deposits	446.96
2.	EMD, rent, temple, etc., deposits	17.21
	Total	464.17

Source: Compiled from Annual Reports.

Processing Unit (Juice and Ice Creams)

The HOPCOMS is preparing fresh fruit juice out of the fruits like grapes, mango, orange, etc., and selling the same to the public at ₹ 8 per 200 ml. Ice cream is also sold at the same point. During the year 2008-09, juice and ice creams turnover was ₹ 80.24 lakh.

Chemical and Fertilisers

HOPCOMS is also supplying inputs to members, such as fertilisers, plant protection chemicals, etc., though it has 11 outlets opened at Bangalore, Sarjapur, Channapatna, Chandapura, Vijyapura, Kolar, Siddighatta, Chikkaballur and Kunigal. During the year 2008-09, the turnover of fertilisers and plant protection chemicals was ₹ 621.74 lakh.

Financial Assistance

For the development of HOPCOMS, *zilla panchayat* provided financial assistance of ₹ 11.97 lakh.

National Horticulture Board (NHB) provided ₹ 28.18 lakh as grants and ₹ 1.08 lakh as loan for construction of each stalls, procurement centers and vehicles. The amount has been utilised for the purpose and the loan was also fully repaid.

Considering the facilities rendered by HOPCOMS during 1990-91, the State Government, National Cooperative Development Corporation (NCDC), sanctioned ₹ 448 lakh for the projects. Under this project, the HOPCOMS constructed 6 central godowns, 21 procurement centres, 165 stalls and purchased of 24 vehicles and installed 1 processing unit. The entire loan amount of ₹ 215 lakh with interest of ₹ 225.54 lakh has been fully repaid by the HOPCOMS.

Agriculture Produce and Marketing Committee (APMC) provided financial assistance of ₹ 10 lakh for the construction of Raitha Bhavan and Stalls.

Marketing Facilities

For the marketing of fruits and vegetables, facilities provided by HOPCOMS are given in Table 8.3.

Table 8.3

Marketing Facilities

S.No.	Particulars	Units	Details
1.	Retail outlets	282	Bangalore urban – 237 Bangalore rural – 15 Kolar – 30
2.	Chemicals and Fertilisers	11	Bangalore District – 5 Kolar District – 5
3.	Cold storage	01	Bangalore Hudson circle
4.	Vehicles	25	Bangalore – 23 Kolar – 02
5.	Processing Units	01	Bangalore Hudson circle
6.	Walk-N-Cooler	02	Bangalore – 1 Kolar – 1
7.	Grading Units	01	Bangalore
8.	Procurement Units	06	Sarjapur, Hoskote, Chennapatna, Kanakapura, Mallur and D.B. Pura
9.	Weigh bridge	01	Bangalore
10.	Storage centres (central godowns)	16	Vegetables – 10 Fruits – 05 Dry fruits – 01

Source: Compiled from Annual Reports.

Institutional Supply (Credit Supply)

Apart from the supplies through retail outlets major institutions, hostels, clubs take bulk supplies to marriage and social functions. Supply details are as below:

S.No.	Name of Districts	Stall	Hospitals	Factories	Hostels, Clubs, Institutions	Total
1.	Bangalore (urban & rural)	252	17	25	44	338
2.	Kolar	30	-	01	03	34
	Total	282	17	26	47	372

Source: Compiled from Annual Reports.

Facilities to Consumers

- Quality fruits and vegetables at reasonable prices.
- Correct weight.
- Retail outlets in expansion.

- Mobile sales.
- Supply of fruits and vegetables to marriages and social functions (free transportation).
- Capital (bulk) supplies to institutions, organisations hostels, hospitals and factories etc.
- Seasonal fruits drinks at reasonable prices (grapes, orange, mango 200 ml).
- Conducting seasonal fruits fare at discount rates (grapes *mela*, mango *mela* and festival *mela*).

Daily Handling of Fruits and Vegetables

The daily handling quantity details are:

- Bangalore: 85 tonnes.
- Kolar: 05 tonnes.
- Total: 90 tonnes.

Future Programmes

- To benefit all grower members and consumers, arrangements be made for market produce.
- Providing technical advise to promote and encourage development of fruits and vegetables.
- Cold chain transportation, cold storage, infrastructure will be created.
- Export of horticulture crops.
- For strengthening of HOPCOMS, proposal under National Horticulture Mission (NHM) has been sanctioned at ₹ 5 crore under R.K.V.Y scheme. Construction of supermarket, modernised godowns and stalls, computerisation of all units, banana ripening chambers, etc.

Year-wise Handling Details (Including all Branches)

The branches of the society, Mysore, Mangalore, Mandya, Hassan and Chikmagalore, were handed over to the respective district horticulture societies in the month of December 2003.

Table 8.4

Year-wise Handling Details

S.No.	Year	Turnover (₹ in lakhs)	Profit	Loss
1.	2003-04	4,366.63		21.36 (-)
2.	2004-05	3,769.18	66.40	
3.	2005-06	3,906.05	57.90	
4.	2006-07 (Tentative)	4,551.31	80.42	
5.	2007-08 (Tentative)	4,850.22	104.11	
6.	2008-09 (April to Aug.) (Tentative)	2,155.50	93.51	

Source: Compiled from Annual Reports.

Analysis

This session presents an analysis of HOPCOMS's functioning and performance. The information presented in this chapter is based on the information gathered from the reports and discussions with the management, employees and various stakeholders of HOPCOMS.

SWOT Analysis

The SWOT analysis of the HOPCOMS is presented below:

Strengths

- Good image among farmers and customers.
- Reasonably good financial position.
- Support from GoK.

Weaknesses

- Limited operations.
- Weak distribution network.
- Focusing only on a few districts of Karnataka.
- Less aggressive in selling.

Opportunities

- Coordinating with other district HOPCOMS will open new vistas.
- Coordination with APMCs and Karnataka State Agricultural Marketing Board (KSAMB) will bring greater advantages.
- Expansion into neighbouring states.
- Market potential in new export markets.

Threats

- Competition from local vendors and organised retailers.
- Heavy competition from local street vendors offering products at the doorstep of the customers.
- Middlemen purchasing the produce right at the farmers' place.
- Lack of awareness among many farmers and customers.
- GoK's ability and willingness to provide continuous support.

Performance Analysis

The performance of the company over the years is presented as follows.

Capital Structure

As at the close of March 31, 2009, the paid-up capital of the company stood at ₹ 264.38 lakh. Out of this, the share of GoK is ₹ 228.09 lakh i.e., 86.2 per cent.

HOPCOMS purchases fruits and vegetables from the farmers, and sells it to customers through its various outlets. The year-wise handling of fruits and vegetables over the years is presented in Table 8.5.

Table 8.5

Year-wise Handling of Fruits and Vegetables

(Qty in MT and Value in lakh)

S. No.	Years	Fruits		Vegetables		Total Handled	
		Qty	Value	Qty	Value	Qty	Value
1	1999	15921	1795	14444	1011	30365	2806
2	2000	15732	1962	16872	1122	32605	3083
3	2001	16384	2041	16659	1244	33043	3284
4	2002	16099	2131	15964	1179	32063	3341
5	2003	14648	1959	14198	1242	28845	3200
6	2004	12565	1681	12903	1103	25468	2484
7	2005	11095	1572	13137	1343	24232	2915
8	2006	10910	1719	14802	1468	25713	3187
9	2007	9869	1757	14274	1659	24144	3416
10	2008	10106	2099	12906	1592	23012	3691

Source: HOPCOMS Reports.

Figure 8.1

Fruits and Vegetables

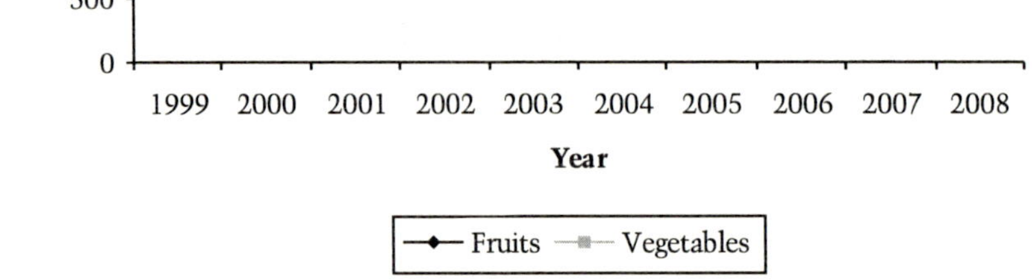

Source: Compiled from Annual Reports.

From Table 8.6, it can be observed that the quantity of fruits and vegetables handled by HOPCOMS is fluctuating. The value of fruits transactions increased from ₹ 1,795 lakh in 1999 to ₹ 2,099 lakh in 2008, registering an increase of 14.48 per cent. The value of fruits sales in 2002 was the maximum with ₹ 2,131 lakh. It was fluctuating in the range of ₹ 1,500-2,200 lakh during 2008-09. The value of vegetables transactions increased from ₹ 1,011 lakh in 1999 to ₹ 1,592 lakh in 2008, registering an increase of 57.47 per cent. The value of vegetables sales was the maximum with ₹ 1,659 lakh in 2007. It was fluctuating between ₹ 1,000 and 1,700 lakh during 2008-09. This indicates the increasing prominence of vegetables.

Financial Performance

The company's income and expenditure during the study under consideration has shown a positive improvement all through the study. The income increased from ₹ 3,126.10 lakh in 2005-06 to ₹ 3,343.80 lakh in 2008-09, registering an increase of 6.96 per cent. The expenditure increased from ₹ 2,973.92 lakh in 2005-06 to ₹ 3,035.31 lakh in 2008-09, registering an increase of 2.1 per cent. The income was more than the expenditure throughout the study period.

Table 8.6

Income and Expenditure of HOPCOMS

(in ₹ lakh)

Time Period	*Income*	*Expenditure*
2005-06	3126.10	2973.92
2006-07	3182.67	3065.13
2007-08	3049.65	2923.02
2008-09	3343.80	3035.31

Source: Compiled from Annual Reports.

Figure 8.2

Income and Expenditure of HOPCOMS

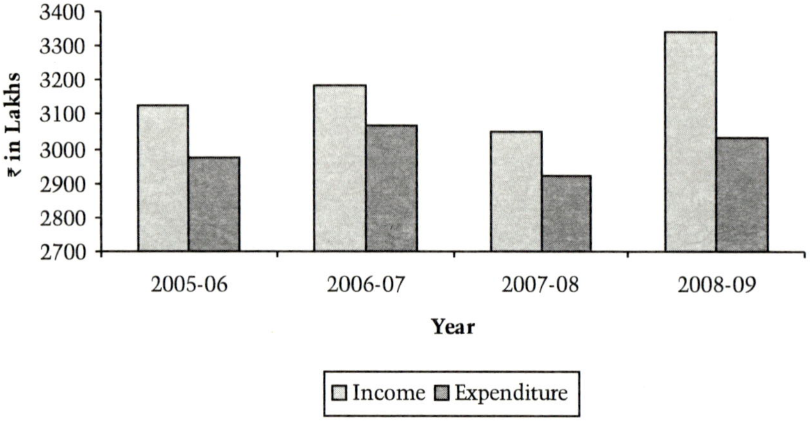

Source: Compiled from Annual Reports.

Turnover

The company's turnover increased from ₹ 3,907.65 lakh in 2005-06 to ₹ 5,512.67 lakh in 2008-09, registering an increase of 41.1 per cent. The turnover of the company showed a steady increase during 2008-09 indicating the effectiveness of the company in attracting the farmers to sell to them and the customers to buy from them.

Table 8.7

Turnover of HOPCOMS

(in ₹ lakh)

S.No.	*Year*	*Turnover*
1.	2005-06	3907.65
2.	2006-07	4510.23
3.	2007-08	4843.28
4.	2008-09	5512.67

Source: Compiled from Annual Reports.

Figure 8.3

Turnover of HOPCOMS

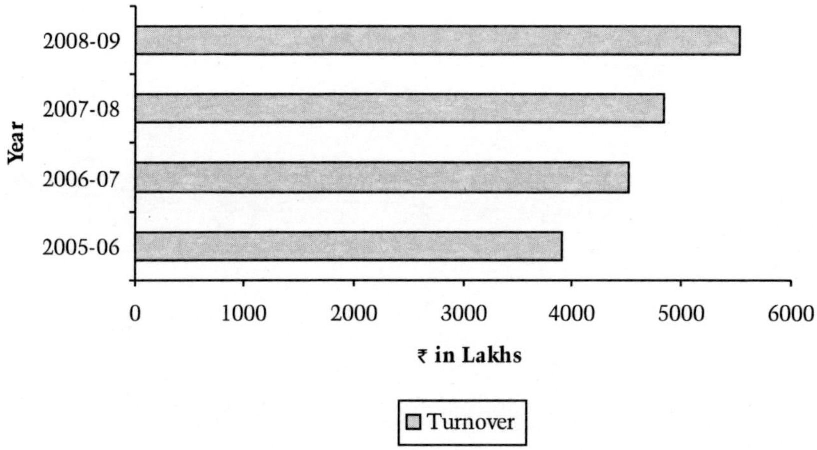

Source: Compiled from Annual Reports.

Liquidity Ratios

Liquidity ratios measure the company's ability to meet its short-term obligations. Liquidity analysis measures how quickly assets are converted into cash. Liquidity ratios also measure the ability to pay off short-term obligations. In day-to-day operations, liquidity management is typically achieved through efficient use of assets. The level of liquidity needed differs from one industry to another. A particular company's liquidity position may also vary according to the anticipated need for funds at any given time. Liquidity ratios reflect a company's position at a point in time and, therefore, use data from the ending balance sheet rather than averages.

The current ratio expresses current assets in relation to current liabilities. Current assets are those assets expected to be consumed or converted into cash within one year, while current liabilities refer to liabilities falling due within one year. A higher ratio indicates high level of liquidity indicating a greater ability to meet short-term obligations. A current ratio of 2:1 is considered to be satisfactory. A lower ratio indicates less liquidity implying a greater reliance on operating cash flow and outside financing to meet short-term obligations. Liquidity affects the company's capacity to take on debt. The current ratio implicitly assumes that inventories and accounts receivable are indeed liquid.

Table 8.8

Liquidity Ratios

Time Period	*Current Ratio*	*Quick Ratio*
2005-06	0.69	0.74
2006-07	0.61	0.64
2007-08	2.43	2.43
2008-09	3.15	3.15

Source: Compiled from Annual Reports.

Figure 8.4

Current Ratio

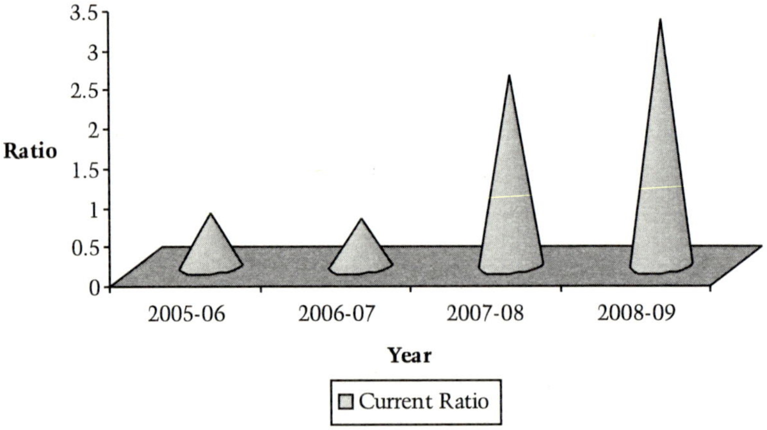

Source: Compiled from Annual Reports.

The current ratio of the company has increased from 0.69 in 2005-06 to 3.15 in 2008-09. The current ratio of the company is increasing every year, indicating the increasing ability of the company to meet its short-term obligations.

Quick ratio is more conservative than the current ratio because it includes only the more liquid current assets in relation to liquid liabilities. A liquid asset is the difference between current assets and stock in trade and prepaid expenses. A liquid liability is the difference between current liabilities and bank overdraft. A higher quick ratio indicates greater liquidity. Liquid ratio reflects the fact that certain assets namely stock in trade/inventories and prepaid expenses cannot usually be converted back into cash easily and quickly. Bank overdraft is not included in current liabilities on the ground. Bank overdraft is generally a permanent way of financing and is not subject to be called on demand. As a rule of thumb, quick ratio of 1:1 is considered satisfactory. It conveys that if quick assets are equal to quick assets then the company is able to meet its short-term obligations. Quick ratio is calculated by taking numerator as quick assets, while denominator as quick liabilities. In absence of bank overdraft, current liabilities are taken instead of quick liabilities.

During the study period, the liquidity position of the company has improved significantly from 0.64 in 2006-07 to 3.15 in 2008-09. But the company's liquidity position is satisfactory because of better management of inventory levels and the company has an excellent liquid position.

Figure 8.5

Quick Ratio

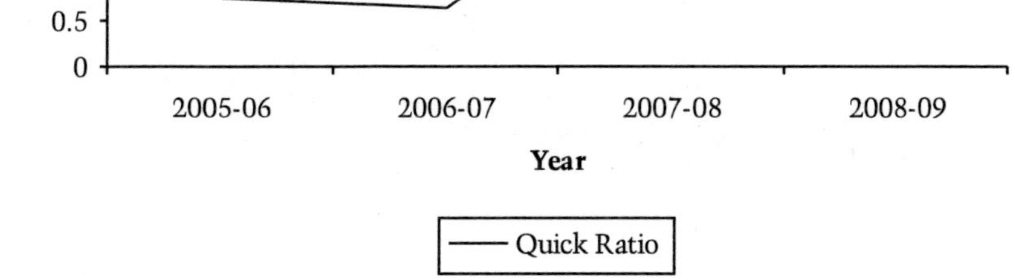

Source: Compiled from Annual Reports.

Long-term Solvency Ratios

Long-term solvency ratios are employed to measure how efficiently the resources i.e., assets of a firm have been managed. These ratios reflect the efficient management of both working capital and long-term assets. It has a direct impact on liquidity and the ability of a company to meet short-term obligations. These ratios are derived from the information provided in the balance sheet item.

The current assets to proprietors funds ratio is the ratio of current assets to the proprietor's funds. Fixed assets to networth ratio is the ratio of fixed assets of the company, which includes buildings, furniture, equipments, etc., to the net worth, which is the shareholders capital. These indicate how well the resources of the company are managed. During the study period, the current asset to proprietors fund ratio has shown marginal increases every year. The fixed assets to networth ratio has also shown marginal increases every year.

Table 8.9

Solvency Ratios

Time Period	*Current Assets to Proprietors Funds Ratio*	*Fixed Assets to Networth Ratio*
2005-06	0.07	1.21
2006-07	0.09	1.27
2007-08	0.37	1.36
2008-09	0.58	1.30

Source: Compiled from Annual Reports.

Figure 8.6

Solvency Ratios

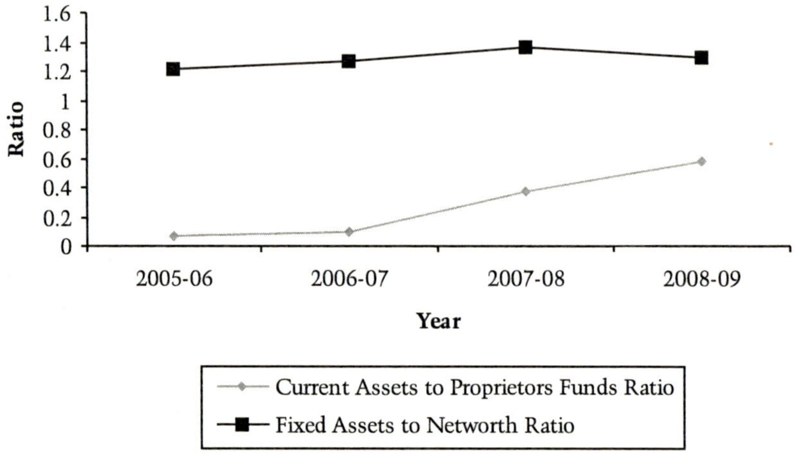

Source: Compiled from Annual Reports.

Profitability Ratios

The ability to generate profit on capital invested is a key determinant of a company's overall value. Profitability reflects company's competitive position in the market and the quality of its management. Profitability ratios measure the return earned by the company during a period. The primary objective of any business undertaking is to earn profits. Profit earning is considered essential for the survival of the business. It is always not correct to emphasise on profit alone, ignoring social corporate responsibility. Profit is considered as essential for expansion and diversification. The investors expect adequate returns on their investments, employees expect better facilities and payments, and creditors want higher security for their interest and loan. A company can discharge its obligations to the various components of the society only through earning of profits. Profitability ratios measure the results of business operations and also measure in overall performance and effectiveness of the firm. It indicates speed with which assets are converted into sales. Profitability ratios are classified into: (i) Profitability in relation to sales and (ii) profitability in relation to investment.

Gross profitability ratio is the ratio of gross profits to sales. During the study period, the gross profitability ratio for the company was fluctuating in the range of 20-25. The net profitability ratio is the ratio of net profits to the sales. During the study period, the net profitability ratio of the company was fluctuating in the range from 1.70 to 3.50.

Table 8.10

Profitability Ratios

Time Period	*Gross Profitability Ratio*	*Net Profitability Ratio*
2005-06	21.84	1.82
2006-07	21.80	2.20
2007-08	20.33	1.70
2008-09	24.29	3.47

Source: Compiled from Annual Reports.

Figure 8.7

Profitability Ratios

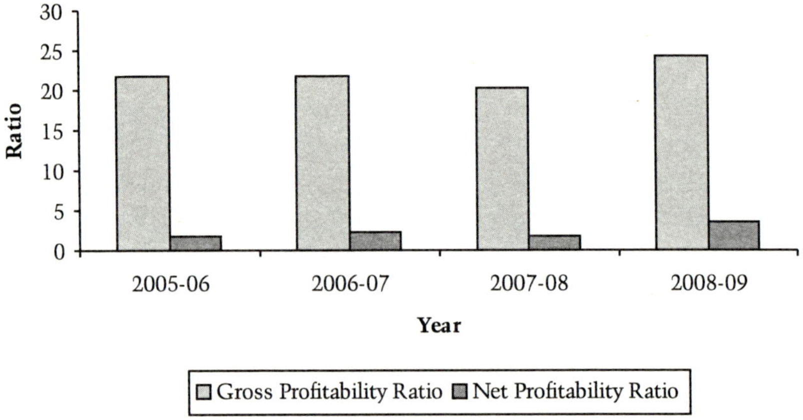

Source: Compiled from Annual Reports.

External Environment Analysis

National Horticulture Board

NHB was set up by Government of India (GoI) in 1984, as an autonomous society under the Societies Registration Act 1860, with a mandate to promote integrated development in horticulture, to help in coordinating, stimulating and sustaining the production and processing of fruits and vegetables and to establish a sound infrastructure in the field of production, processing and marketing with a focus on post-harvest management to reduce losses.

Objectives of NHB

The broad objectives are:

- To develop high quality horticultural farms in identified belts and make such areas vibrant with horticultural activity, which in turn will act as hubs for developing commercial horticulture.
- To develop post-harvest management infrastructure.
- To strengthen Market Information System and horticulture database.

- To assist R&D programmes to develop products suited for specific varieties with improved methods and horticulture technology.
- To provide training and education to farmers and processing industry personnel for improving agronomic practices and new technologies.
- To promote consumption of fruits/vegetables in fresh and processed form, etc.

Organisational Structure

Board of Directors

An apex body known as Board of Directors supervises the Management of NHB, which is headed by Union Agriculture Minister as its President and Union Minister of State for Agriculture as its Vice-President. The other members of the board are as follows:

- Secretary, Department of Agriculture & Cooperation (DAC) (Ex-Officio)
- Director General, Indian Council of Agricultural Research (Ex-Officio)
- Horticulture Commissioner, DAC (Ex-Officio)
- Financial Advisor, DAC (Ex-Officio)
- Chairman, Agriculture & Processed Food Products Export Development Authority (APEDA) (Ex-Officio)
- Executive Director, NHB (Ex-Officio)
- Eight representatives in horticulture industry representing the interests of cooperative societies, leading horticulturists and leading exporters of horticulture produce (to be nominated by State Government).
- A representative each of food processing industry, Ministry of Shipping and Transport, Ministry of Railways, Ministry of Civil Aviation and Tourism or any other ministry who may be invited specially with the consent of the President (Ex-Officio).

Managing Committee

The managing Committee is headed by the Union Secretary (DAC) as its Chairman. It has been assigned the role of general superintendence, direction and control over the affairs and functions of the board. The composition of the managing committee is as under:

- Secretary (DAC) Chairman.
- Additional Secretary/Special Secretary Incharge of Horticulture, DAC Member.
- Advisor (Agriculture) Planning Commission or his representative Member.
- Financial Advisor, DAC Member.
- Chairman, Agriculture & Processed Products Export development Authority Member.
- Horticulture Commissioner, DAC Member.
- General Manager, National Bank for Agriculture and Rural Development (NABARD) Member.
- Managing Director NHB, Member Secretary.

Principal Executive

The Managing Director is the Principal Executive of NHB.

Rythu Bazaars

Concept

Andhra Pradesh is the second largest producer of fruits, vegetables and flowers in the country. The predominantly grown fruit crops are mango, banana, cashew nuts, sapota, guava and pomegranate. Brinjal, lady fingers, onions, tomatoes, beans and gourds are the major vegetables produced in the state.

Regulated market yards for fruits and vegetables are functioning only at few centres in the state. The marketing system for fruits and vegetables is in the hands of middlemen. Middlemen exist at various levels between the farmer and the consumer and exploit through malpractices in weighments, handling and payments.

The farmer's share in the consumer's rupee is estimated to be just 40 paise. In addition, the estimated losses in handling vegetables through the traditional channel of marketing are about 30-35 per cent. Large numbers of small farmers are unable to effectively bargain for a better price in the wholesale markets. Inefficiencies in wholesale markets result in a long chain of intermediaries, multiple handling, and loss in quality and increase the gap between producer and consumer. Intermediaries and system inefficiencies consume a disproportionate share of consumer prices. Large number of small retailers, each handling small quantities, create high overheads leading to high margins on produce.

It was, therefore, felt necessary to evolve an alternate marketing strategy, where both growers and consumers are benefited through Rythu Bazaars. Rythu Bazaars are, thus, planned for direct interface between the farmers and the consumers eliminating middlemen. Rythu Bazaars are acting as price stabilisation centres in the state. Rythu Bazaars operate outside the purview of agricultural market committees and are managed by estate officers and under the control of joint collectors.

Objectives

The objectives are:

- To ensure remunerative prices to the farmers and provide fresh vegetables to consumers at reasonable rates fixed everyday.
- To facilitate prompt realisation of sale proceeds to farmers without any deductions.
- To curb malpractices in weighments, providing vegetables with correct weighments to consumers.
- To provide direct interface between farmers and consumers eliminating intermediaries in trade.

Location of Rythu Bazaars

Rythu Bazaars are located on government lands identified by the district collectors. The location shall have to be convenient, both for the farmers and consumers. The criteria for opening of new Rythu Bazaars is to have at least one acre of land in strategic location and identification of 250 vegetable-growing farmers.

Infrastructure Facilities

The required infrastructure is provided in all Rythu Bazaars with funds from agricultural market committees. The temporary structures in Rythu Bazaars are replaced by semi-permanent structures to provide adequate protection against sun/rain to the producers and the users alike.

The Rythu Bazaars ensure:

- Adequate number of sheds for farmers to sell their produce.
- Adequate arrangements for supply of drinking water.
- Toilet facilities with proper sanitation.
- Proper arrangements for parking of vehicles.
- Arrangements for removal of garbage and cleaning the market by local body.
- Facilities for storage of unsold produce like zero energy cool chambers.
- Weighing scales to all the farmers with proper arrangements for issue and collection.

Villages

The farmers from a cluster of 10-15 predominantly vegetable-growing villages are identified, so as to enable provision of horticulture services, inputs and transportation arrangements to the Rythu Bazaars effectively. Horticulture Department identifies such clusters for all the Rythu Bazaars.

Farmers

Identification of farmers is done jointly by a team consisting of:

- Mandal revenue officer (MRO).
- Horticulture officer/consultant.
- Agricultural officer, in the villages.

The team finalises the schedule of visits to the villages and publicises it adequately among the vegetable-growing farmers. As per the schedule, the team visits the villages and convenes a meeting of vegetable-growing farmers. In the meeting, they explain about the advantages of the Rythu Bazaars to the farmers through provision of:

- Horticultural services.
- Seed supply at subsidised rates.
- Transportation arrangements.
- Price mechanism.
- Elimination of middlemen to motivate them to reap the benefits.

After the meeting, the team visits fields of the willing farmers and issue temporary identity cards on the spot. Temporary identity cards issued shall be replaced by laminated photo identity cards within a week. Tenants are also given identity cards on field verification. Farmers can also form groups as per their choice. Each group can send one or more members on rotation for sale of vegetables in Rythu Bazaars. They will also be extended the benefits given to the self-help groups (SHGs) by the government.

Allotment of Shops to Farmers by Estate Officer

Only the farmers/groups with valid photo identity cards will be allowed to sell in Rythu Bazaar. The daily allotment of shops shall be on 'first come first serve' (FCFS) basis on rotation. No one shall be allowed to occupy the same shop continuously. Farmers will not be allowed to reserve the shop by keeping vegetables at night.

Preventing the Entry of Middlemen

The entry of middlemen (retailers/wholesalers) defeats the purpose of setting of Rythu Bazaars. No seller will be allowed to enter into Rythu Bazaar without valid photo identity card. The bogus identity cards shall be cancelled immediately. Deterrent action shall against the persons responsible for issuing cards to ineligible persons. Estate officer will be held responsible for allowing persons without proper identity cards. There shall be frequent surprise inspections by joint collector and others, leaving their remarks in the inspection register without fail.

Price Fixation

The price fixation in Rythu Bazaars shall be through a committee of farmers and the estate officer. The prices generally in Rythu Bazaars shall have to be 25 per cent above the wholesale rates and 25 per cent less than the local retail price. Marketing department shall provide the wholesale prices to estate officer for realistic price fixation. Estate officer should also make his efforts to obtain the wholesale and retail prices. Whenever Marketing Department is not able to provide wholesale prices by 6.00 A.M. in the morning, previous day's wholesale price may be used. For the different varieties (clearly distinguishable) of the same vegetable, different sale price may be fixed. The estate officers shall ensure that prices are displayed prominently at strategic locations.

Lease of Structures/Parking Space

Rythu Bazaars can generate sufficient income for maintenance through auction of parking space, canteen, etc. Joint collector is the competent authority for finalisation of auction. The money released by way of auction shall be credited to Rythu Bazaar funds and the funds can be used for the purpose of :

- Sanitation.
- Drinking water facilities.
- Purchase and repairs of weighing scales, and maintenance of Rythu Bazaars.

The estate officers shall maintain proper accounts/cash books, etc.

Duties of the Estate Officers

The Estate Officers are responsible for:

- Upkeep and maintenance of Rythu Bazaars.
- Daily allotment of space on FCFS basis.
- Provision allotment of weighing scales to farmers daily and collecting them back in the evening.
- Formation of price fixation committees.

- Convening of the price fixation committee meetings everyday in morning for realistic price fixation.
- Price fixation.
- Ensure sales at the prices fixed.
- Conducting a meeting of all farmers once in a week to assess the functioning and to take course corrections and send the minutes to joint collector and director of marketing.
- Prominent display of prices at strategic points.
- Use of public address system for announcement of prices.
- Prevention of entry of middlemen.
- Cleanliness/sanitation.
- Proper supply of power and water.
- Proper transport facilities to the farmers.
- Proper recording of daily arrivals and sales.
- Prompt furnishing of returns and reports to the joint collectors/ director of marketing.
- Encourage sale of vegetables not grown locally by the SHGs.
- Ensure that the farmers sell vegetables mentioned in the temporary identity card issued by the Estate Officer.
- Coordinate with horticulture officers/consultants in timely distribution of seed material/inputs to promote horticulture production.
- Prevent entry of anti-social elements especially at night.
- Proper maintenance of accounts and inspection register.
- Settle disputes arising on account of quality, price, etc., between sellers and purchasers.
- Lease of space for parking/canteen, etc., and realisation of lease amounts.
- Organise proper watch and ward.
- Prompt action on adverse news items relating to Rythu Bazaars.

- Problems of transportation, middlemen, requirement of additional infrastructure and other problems to be taken to the notice of joint collectors as and when necessary.

Conclusions and Suggestions

Conclusions

The following conclusions can be drawn on the basis of the analysis.

- The operations of the HOPCOMS are generating profits every year.
- The company has good image in the minds of the customers and farmers.
- The company has reasonably good financial position.
- The value of fruits transactions increased from ₹ 1,795 lakh in 1999 to ₹ 2,099 lakh in 2008, registering an increase of 14.48 per cent. It was fluctuating in the range of ₹ 1,500-2,200 lakh during 2008-09.
- The value of vegetables transactions increased from ₹ 1,011 lakh in 1999 to ₹ 1,592 lakh in 2008, registering an increase of 57.47 per cent. It was fluctuating between ₹ 1,000-1,700 lakh during 2008-09. This indicates that the increasing prominence of vegetables.
- The income increased from ₹ 3,126.10 lakh in 2005-06 to ₹ 3,343.80 lakh in 2008-09, registering an increase of 6.96 per cent.
- The expenditure increased from ₹ 2,973.92 lakh in 2005-06 to ₹ 3,035.31 lakh in 2008-09, registering an increase of 2.1 per cent. The income was more than the expenditure through the study period.
- The company's turnover increased from ₹ 3,907.65 lakh in 2005-06 to ₹ 5,512.67 lakh in 2008-09, registering an increase of 41.1 per cent.

- The turnover of the company showed a steady increase during 2008-09 indicating the effectiveness of the company in attracting the farmers to sell to them and the customers to buy from them.
- The current ratio of the company is increasing every year, indicating the increasing ability of the company to meet its short-term obligations.
- The liquidity position of the company has improved significantly with the quick ratio improving from 0.64 in 2006-07 to 3.15 in 2008-09.
- The current asset to proprietors fund ratio has shown marginal increases every year. The fixed assets to networth ratio has also shown marginal increases every year.
- The gross profitability ratio for the company is fluctuating in the range of 20-25. The net profitability ratio of the company is fluctuating in the range from 1.70 to 3.50.
- The operations of the company are limited to a few districts in Karnataka.
- There is heavy competition from local street vendors selling vegetables at the doorsteps of the customers.
- There is lack of awareness among many farmers about the company and its activities.
- Many farmers sell their produce to middlemen who purchase it at the farmers' places.
- The organised competitors like Reliance Fresh operate on a bigger scale covering larger areas.
- In the neighbouring state of Andhra Pradesh, government has set up Rythu Bazaars to facilitate the farmers to sell their produce.
- The revenues for farmers at Rythu Bazaar is nearly 20-25 per cent more than the open market prices. The revenues for farmers at HOPCOMS are nearly 10-15 per cent more than the open market prices.

- The Rythu Bazaars facilitate the bringing together of farmers and customers at one place by eliminating middlemen and also with fixation of prices.
- HOPCOMS does not facilitate bringing together of farmers and customers. It buys from farmers and sells to the customers.
- HOPCOMS plays a key role in stabilising the market by controlling the prices.
- It is employing nearly 1,000 people directly and around three times the number, indirectly.

Suggestions

The following suggestions are offered for consideration by GoK:

- HOPCOMS's success depends upon the fruit and vegetable farmers. It should initiate awareness programmes in the villages, so that more and more farmers become members and sell their produce at HOPCOMS.
- Toll-free telephone numbers can be introduced at HOPCOMSs centres for disseminating information to the farmers easily.
- The company should expand its scope of operations by coordinating with district HOPCOMS on the lines of Milk Federations.
- The company should explore the possibilities of entering new markets.
- The company should try to reach out to the customers by opening more outlets and teaming up with local vendors.
- The company has relevance/need in the present context. Hence, government should continue with the organisation.
- Government can adopt the Rythu Bazaar concept of Andhra Pradesh, in places where the HOPCOMS are weak.

9 Karnataka State Agricultural Marketing Board

V. Srikanth

Introduction

The Karnataka State Agricultural Marketing Board (KSAMB) was established on September 1972 as per section 100 of Karnataka Agricultural Produce Marketing (Regulation) [KAPM(R)] Act, 1966, and Rules, 1968. The Board acts as a liaison agency between the market committees and Government of Karnataka (GoK) for all-round development of agricultural marketing in the state.

Functions

The important functions of the Board are enumerated in sections 111 and 112 of the KAPM(R) Act, 1966. They are as follows:

- Promote grading and standardisation of agricultural produce.
- Assist for general improvement of the regulation of marketing in the state.
- Giving aid to financially weak (or needy) market committees in the form of loans and grants.
- Propaganda and publicity on matters relating to regulated marketing of agricultural produce.
- Imparting education in regulated marketing of agricultural produce.
- General improvement of the facilities for the transport of notified agricultural produce and the marketing thereof.
- Training the officers and staff of marketing committees in the state.

- Advise on matters referred to it by state government.
- To coordinate functioning of all the market committees with the help of information service obtained by both national and international market.
- To arrange for safety insurance on the life of farmers and if necessary contribute towards premium payable in respect of all agriculturists in the state.
- To arrange or organise seminars, workshops or exhibitions on subject relating to agricultural marketing.

Constitution

The Board consists of one representative from each revenue district of the state. The member shall be a chairman of the market committee in the district, elected by an electorate consisting of the chairmen of all the market committees in a district. The Hon'ble Minister in-charge of Agricultural Produce Marketing shall be the Ex-Officio Chairman of the Board. Secretary to government, cooperation department or his nominee, principal secretary to government, agriculture department or his nominee shall be the Ex-officio members of the Board. The Director of Agricultural Marketing shall be the official member of the Board. The Director, Department of Agricultural Marketing, GoK, is the Ex-Officio Managing Director of the Board. The Board shall elect a Vice-Chairman from among the elected 29 members of the Board.

Financial Source

The main source of income to the Board is as follows:

- Contribution by the market committee in the state at 5 per cent of the gross receipts by way of market fee and licence fee every month.
- Grant by State Government at 1 per cent of the gross receipts by way of market fee and licence fee realised in every year by the Agriculture Produce Marketing Committee (APMCs).

Organisation

There are five wings in the Board namely:

- Administrative wing.
- Research wing.
- Board divisional offices.
- Training wing.
- Printing and publication wing.

Administrative Wing

Chief General Manager heads this wing. The Administrative Wing coordinates the activities of all the different wings of the Board. The important activities looked after by the Administrative Wing are: monitoring of the budget; conducting board meetings, matters relating to sanction and release of loans; providing computer-related solutions to the day-to-day functioning of the Department and also to the APMCs of the state. The wing does the overall supervision of all the wings of the Board.

The Computer Wing attached to the Administrative Wing is fully engaged in collection and dissemination of market information pertaining to arrivals, sales, minimum, maximum, model prices and value of important notified agricultural commodities. Information regarding 134 notified agricultural commodities is being downloaded from Maratavahini website. Based on this, primary data, weekly and monthly reports are being generated and sent to Director of Agricultural Marketing, GoK; Development Commissioner and Ex-officio Commissioner, Agricultural Production, GoK; Secretary to Government, Department of Co-operation, GoK; Commissioner for Food and Civil Supplies, GoK; Secretary to Government, Food, Civil Supplies and Consumer Affairs, GoK. Apart from this, data pertaining to agricultural marketing is being supplied to University of Agricultural Sciences, National Horticultural Board; Directorate of Marketing and Inspection, Government of India; Bangalore Unit, Cotton Corporation of India (GoI), Coimbatore and Bangalore etc.; and desired users.

Research Wing

- This wing is engaged in conducting research pertaining to several aspects of agricultural marketing and allied subjects. So far, 320 various research reports have been prepared. These reports include appraisal reports to seek financial assistance for the development of market yards by National Bank for Agriculture and Rural Development (NABARD), establishment of special commodity markets for fruits and vegetables, survey reports for the establishment of main and sub-markets and also amalgamation of markets, establishment of pre-cooling units, cold storages in the state. The research wing of the Board is mainly undertaking the problem-oriented research confronted by the market committees in their day-to-day activities.
- A detailed project report on development of 29 rural markets under Rural Infrastructure Development Fund (RIDF) with an estimated cost of ₹ 4.45 crore has been sanctioned by NABARD during 2001.
- The Research Wing is preparing the annual work plan to get grants from GoI for agricultural marketing improvement.
- During November 2001, the Board has entered into an Memorandum of Understanding (MoU) with University of Agricultural Sciences at Bangalore and Dharwar, to undertake research and extension work. The research wing carries out necessary coordination work.

Board Divisional Offices

- In order to popularise the importance of regulated markets in rural areas, the following extension activities are taken up by the divisional offices:
    - Participation in various exhibitions that are being held in the state to exhibit the agricultural marketing activities with special reference to regulation of trade, facilities available in APMCs, etc.
    - Organising film shows on agricultural marketing in rural areas.

- Advertising the advantages of regulation of agricultural produce through All India Radio (AIR), TV and other media.
- Production of documentary films on matters relating to agricultural marketing. In this connection, the Board produced short films.
- Participating in cattle fair for awarding gold medals to the best adjudged cattle.
- Organising district level workshops for undertaking extension activities related to agricultural marketing.
- Extending all other necessary facilities to undertake various studies on agricultural marketing.

• As per the recent restructure, the divisional offices are responsible for implementing the schemes such as Raitha Sanjeevini, Janashree Vima Yojana for Hamals, apart from other different schemes of the Board relating to APMCs coming under the respective divisions.

Training Wing

The Board has established two training centres at Mysore and Hubli. The training courses conducted in these centres are as follows:

• Refreshers Course for Secretaries and Assistant Secretaries of Marketing Committee.

- Accountancy and Auditing Course.
- Graders Training Course.
- Training Course on Market Intelligence.
- Training Course for Members of Market Committee.
- Office Procedures Training Course.
- Farmers Training Course.
- Training Course for the Members of *Gram Panchayats*.
- Training Course on Developmental Works.
- Farmers Training through Radio Lessons.

- Coordinated Training Programme with National Institute of Agricultural Marketing (NIAM) and other Institutions.
  - Training on legal reforms for the APMC Chairmen/Officers.
  - Training on Warehousing Storage and Rural Godowns for the officials of Central Warehousing Corporation (CWC), State Warehousing Corporation (SWC) and APMCs.
  - Grading, Standardisation and Quality Control for the officials of APMC, Food and Civil Supplies and Agriculture Department.
  - Training on Information Technology (IT) for the Officers of Agricultural Marketing Department/Board.
  - Training on Post-Harvest management for progressive farmers.
  - Training on Export Promotion for progressive farmers and Cooperative Societies.
  - Training on Market Infrastructure Development and private participation for the officers and the engineers of Market Development Project, Department of Agricultural Marketing.

Printing and Publication Wing

Printing Wing

In order to bring out the uniform printing of receipts, registers, etc., used in the APMCs, the Board has established a printing press at Hubli with latest printing machinery. *Krishipete* monthly journal in Kannada is printed in this press. This press also meets the printing requirements of all the APMCs in the state.

Publication Wing

The Board is publishing a monthly journal exclusively devoted to agricultural marketing in Kannada entitled *Krishipete* from December 1974. Circulation of the magazine has crossed 25,000 prints per month. The magazine contains articles written by the experts in the field of agricultural marketing and allied subjects. The journal is used to publicise the activities of the Department of Agricultural Marketing, Marketing Board, APMCs and other activities related to agricultural marketing.

Loans for Developmental Works

The Board sanctioned loan to market committees to undertake developmental works in market yards. The Board has also given loans for link roads. The following table shows the loan amount sanctioned to different APMCs in the state towards developmental works and towards link roads.

Table 9.1

Loan Amount Sanctioned to Different APMCs

S. No.	*Purpose*	*Loan Amount Sanctioned*
1.	Developmental works	13.26 crore
2.	Formation of Link Roads	4.85 crore
	Total	18.11 crore

Source: Compiled from Annual Reports.

Organising of Seminars

The Board is organising district level, state level and national level seminars. These seminars are organised by the respective divisional level offices of the Board as a part of extension activities.

Floor Price Scheme for Agriculture/Horticulture Commodities in Karnataka

To ensure price stability in the agriculture sector, it is necessary to ensure remunerative prices for the farmers' produce. It is, with this objective that Floor Prices Scheme for agricultural commodities in Karnataka has been implemented. To protect the interests of the farmers against distress sale of agricultural commodities, by assuring a floor price, the Agricultural Policy Resolution of GoK stressed to bring in 'price and market reforms' in the agricultural sector of the state. The scheme shall be applicable in the whole state of Karnataka and to notified agricultural and horticultural commodities grown in the state. So far ₹ 665.14 crore have been released to different purchase agencies and 3,51,211 farmers are benefited under this scheme.

Welfare Schemes

The Board is implementing the following welfare schemes for the benefit of farmers and market functionaries.

Raitha Sanjeevani: This is an accident benefit scheme implemented by the Board from 1996. Under this scheme, a farmer who meets with an accident and dies while performing agricultural operations in the field is sanctioned a sum of ₹ 50,000 by the Board. The immediate dependent has to apply through the APMC for the sanction of the amount. In case of permanent disability, the victim gets the financial assistance from board as follows:

- Accidental death - ₹ 50,000.00
- Loss of 2 hands and 2 limbs - ₹ 15,000.00
- Loss of eyes - ₹ 12,000.00
- Loss of 1 hand or 1 limb - ₹ 7,500.00
- Loss of 1 eye - ₹ 6,000.00
- Loss of finger of hand or legs (per finger) - ₹ 1,500.00
- Broken waist - ₹ 15,000.00

So far, 5,593 claims have been settled and the amount ₹ 13.06 crore is distributed.

Janashree Vima Yojana for Weighmen, Hamals and Cartmen: The Board is implementing an insurance scheme for the benefit of 16,000 licensed weighmen, *hamals* and cartmen working in different APMCs of Karnataka, since 1994. During 2007-08, 15,254 persons enrolled in the scheme and 117 persons were benefited from this scheme. The total amount paid during 2007-08, towards compensation was ₹ 42.90 lakh. So far, 1,272 persons are benefited in this scheme. The details are as follows:

- Natural death ₹ 30,000.00
- Accidental death ₹ 75,000.00
- Permanent disability ₹ 75,000.00
- Permanent loss of
2 eyes
2 limbs
2 hands ₹ 75,000.00
- Loss of 1 eye, 1 hand ₹ 37,500.00

In addition to this, GoI pays scholarship to two students of 9th to 12th standard in a family of the insurer and they get a sum of ₹ 300 per quarter.

Analysis

This section presents an analysis of KSAMB's functioning and performance. The information presented in this section is based on the information gathered from the reports and discussions with the management, employees and various stakeholders of KSAMB.

SWOT Analysis

The SWOT analysis of the KSAMB is presented below:

Strengths

- Highly knowledgeable and qualified senior management.
- Accumulated vast knowledge, information and capabilities with relation to agriculture.
- Vast experience in executing minimum support price (MSP) programmes.
- Good systems for collection, management and dissemination of relevant information.
- Support from GoK.

Weaknesses

- Plays a passive and advisory role.
- Poor coordination with APMC resulting in poor implementation.
- Heavily dependent on APMC for revenues.
- Ineffective publicity to farmers.
- Lack of awareness among farmers about KSAMB.

Opportunities

- KSAMB and APMC are working under the same Director, who can bring about role clarity and more coordination.
- Effective implementation of welfare schemes can create tremendous goodwill and confidence among the farmers.

- Continuous and effective training to the employees and the farmers can bring about awareness and increase the effectiveness.
- Adoption of new, yet, farmer friendly technologies.

Threats

- New farming and marketing technologies.
- Increasing choice to the farmers to market their produce.
- Dependence on APMCs for revenues.

Performance Analysis

The income and expenditure figures of KSAMB over the years are presented in Table 9.2.

Table 9.2

Overview of Income and Expenditure

(₹ in lakh)

Income/Expenditure for the year	*2003-04*	*2004-05*	*2005-06*	*2006-07*	*2007-08*	*2008-09*
Income						
APMC Contribution	407.59	387.96	447.52	521.85	622.15	722.49
Govt. Grant	51.00	50.00	----	103.90	54.08	27.04
Interest on APMC Loans	30.62	27.41	11.32	9.71	19.86	14.59
Interest on FDRs	5.99	8.01	10.12	12.02	6.42	22.28
Miscellaneous Receipts	1.92	----	6.81	3.49	11.81	3.05
Building Rent	8.72	6.41	8.58	8.88	53.85	53.04
Group Insurance Scheme	2.45	1.56	1.54	1.42	1.28	1.64
Raitha Sanjeevani Scheme	58.06	102.00	129.00	113.80	206.50	263.00
Printing Press Income	93.01	92.68	85.01	89.02	110.76	125.86
Krishipete Mag. Income	20.35	20.64	21.69	23.11	27.24	44.45
Total	281.56	408.27	295.81	288.15	617.41	613.82
Expenditure:						
Employees Compensation	229.99	214.95	242.03	256.14	325.32	375.14
Raitha Sanjeevani Scheme	115.50	126.55	112.09	170.39	235.40	337.50
Training Expenses	4.99	5.37	3.45		69.79	2.68
Printing Press Expenditure	55.84	57.09	55.32	53.55	74.64	71.25
Krishipete Mag. Expenses	23.99	19.01	20.28	27.44	24.48	25.43
Total	635.37	729.49	743.58	824.36	996.36	1060.10
Income/Expenditure	(353.81)	(321.22)	(447.77)	(536.21)	(378.95)	(446.28)

Source: KSAMB Reports.

The company's income and expenditure during the study under consideration has shown both the income and expenditure increasing almost every year. During the year 2003-04, the income was ₹ 281.56 lakh, while for the year 2008-09, the income was ₹ 613.82 lakh, registering an increase of 118 per cent. The expenditure was more than the income throughout the study period.

Table 9.3

Income and Expenditure

(₹ in lakh)

Time Period	*Income*	*Expenditure*
2003-04	281.56	635.37
2004-05	408.27	729.49
2005-06	295.81	743.58
2006-07	288.15	824.36
2007-08	617.41	996.36
2008-09	613.82	1060.10

Source: Compiled from Annual Reports.

Figure 9.1

Income and Expenditure

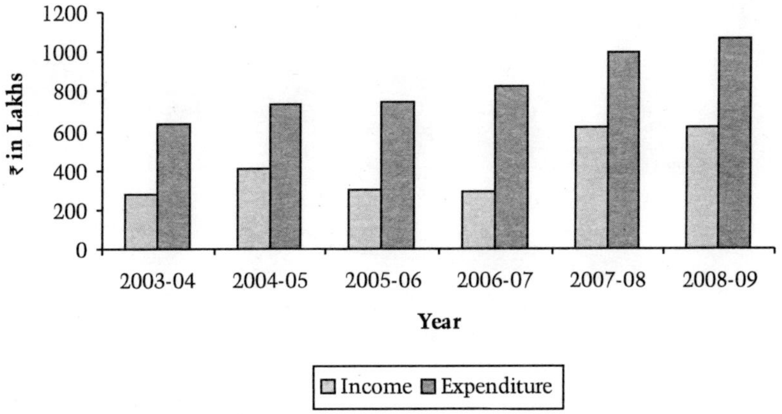

Source: Compiled from Annual Reports.

The expenditure during the year 2003-04 was ₹ 635.37 lakh, while for the year 2008-09, the expenditure was ₹ 1,060.10 lakh, showing an increase of 66.84 per cent.

Among the various heads of expenditure, employee compensation is the major head. Employee compensation has increased from ₹ 229.99 lakh in 2003-04 to ₹ 375.14 lakh in 2008-09, registering an increase of 63.1 per cent over the years.

Table 9.4

Employee Compensation

(₹ in lakh)

Year	Employee Compensation
2003-04	229.99
2004-05	214.95
2005-06	242.03
2006-07	256.14
2007-08	325.32
2008-09	375.14

Source: Compiled from Annual Reports.

Figure 9.2

Employee Compensation

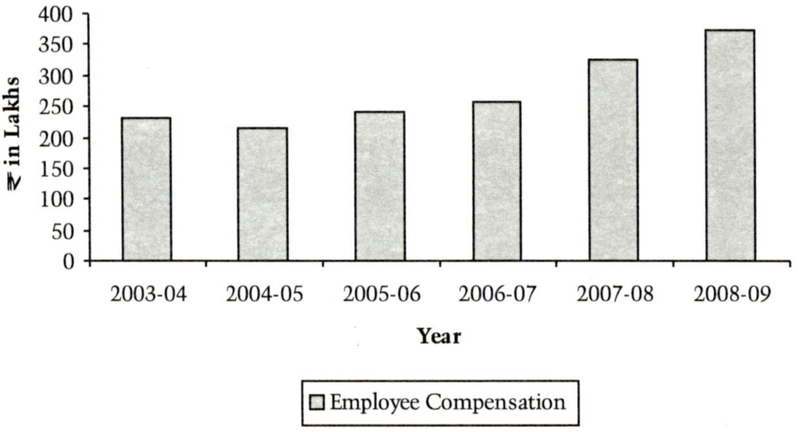

Source: Compiled from Annual Reports.

One of the major acitvities pursued by KSAMB is the implementation of welfare schemes for the benefit of farmers and market functionaries. Raitha Sanjeevani is one such welfare scheme. Through this scheme, a large number of farmers are getting benefit and is one of the major heads of expenditure for the company.

Table 9.5

Raitha Sanjeevani

(₹ in Lakh)

Year	*Raitha Sanjeevani*
2003-04	115.50
2004-05	126.55
2005-06	112.09
2006-07	170.39
2007-08	235.40
2008-09	337.50

Source: Compiled from Annual Reports.

The expenditure for the company under the Raitha Sanjeevani scheme has increased from ₹ 115.50 lakh in 2003-04 to ₹ 337.50 lakh in 2008-09, an increase of 192.2 per cent. This indicates the popularity of this scheme among the farmers and the members.

Figure 9.3

Raitha Sanjeevani

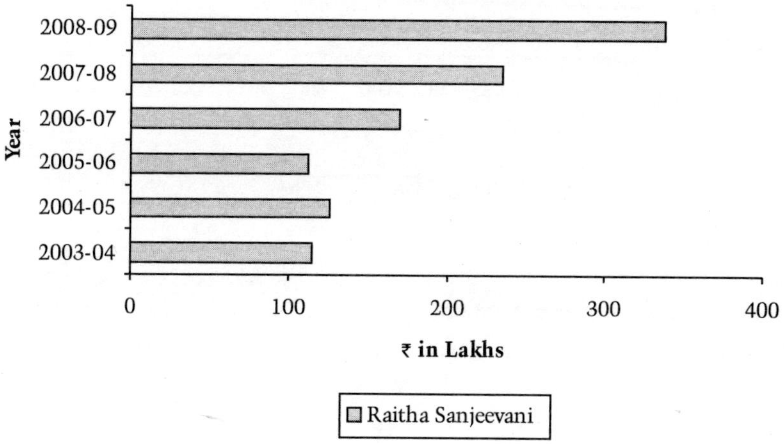

Source: Compiled from Annual Reports.

Amongst the sources of income for KSAMB, the contributions from APMCs is the major one. The market committees in the state contribute 5 per cent of the gross receipts by way of market fee and license fee, every month to the company.

Table 9.6

APMC Contributions

(₹ in Lakh)

Year	APMC Contributions
2003-04	407.59
2004-05	387.96
2005-06	447.52
2006-07	521.85
2007-08	622.15
2008-09	722.49

Source: Compiled from Annual Reports.

Figure 9.4

APMC Contributions

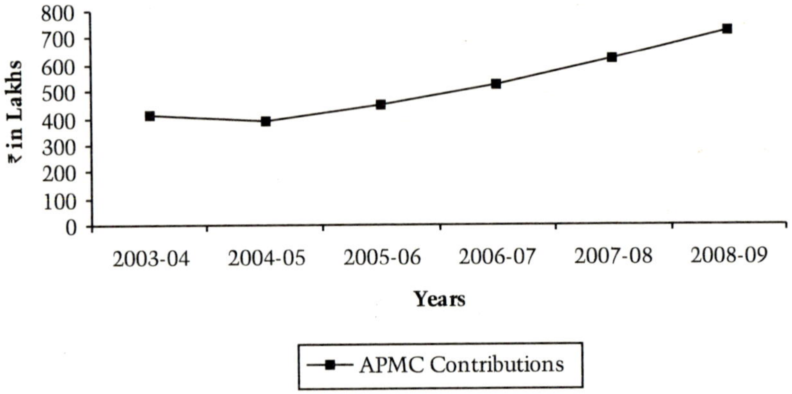

Source: Compiled from Annual Reports.

From Table 9.6, it can be observed that the contributions to the Board through APMCs have been continuously increasing every year except 2003-04. It has increased from ₹ 407.59 lakh in 2003-04 to ₹ 722.49 lakh in 2008-09, an increase of 77.25 per cent.

External Environment Analysis

Punjab State Agricultural Marketing Board (PSAMB) was established on May 26, 1961, under the Punjab Agricultural Produce Markets Act, 1961, with an objective to control and supervise the marketing network of sale, purchase, storage and processing of processed or non-processed agricultural produce so notified from agricultural, horticulture, animal husbandry and forest produce. PSAMB is a corporate body as well as a local authority having perpetual succession and a common seal, with power to acquire, hold and sell property.

There are 145 agricultural produce market committees in the state established under the Act. There are one principal market yard, one or more sub-market yards and seasonal purchase centres in each market committee. During the marketing season for the wheat in *rabi* and paddy in *kharif*, about 1590 and 1514 purchase centres are established apart from the main principal market yards and sub-market yards that facilitate the farmer to sell his produce within the radius of six to eight kilometers. PSAMB exercises superintendence and control over the APMC's.

Objective

The Punjab agriculture produce is being regulated under the Punjab Agriculture Produce Markets Act, 1961. The preamble of the act is "An act to consolidate and amend the law relating to the better regulation of the purchase, sale, storage and processing of Agricultural produce and the establishment of the markets for Agricultural produces in the state of Punjab." The primary object of Punjab Mandi Board and Market Committees is to establish modern markets for efficient marketing of agricultural produce by providing modern facilities in the *mandis* and to enforce the provisions of the act, rules and bye-laws framed there under. PSAMB is a body corporate as well as a local authority by the name of the State Agricultural Marketing Board, having perpetual succession and a common seal, with power, subject to the provisions of this Act, to acquire and hold property and shall by the said name sue and be sued.

Whereas, market committees are to enforce the provisions of this Act and the rules and the bye-laws made thereunder in the notified market area and, when so required by the Board, to establish a market therein, providing such facilities for persons visiting it in connection with the purchase, sale, storage, weighing and processing of agricultural produce concerned. The Board may from time to time direct these market committees to control and regulate the admission to the markets. Market committees are service rendering agencies and their main source of income is market fee. The existing rate of market fee on purchase or sale transactions of all agricultural produce specified in the schedule is 2 per cent. Timber and firewood has recently been added in the schedule of the Act and 0.50 per cent fee is levied on the purchase or sale of the same. In addition to this, the state government has also levied 2 per cent rural development fund on the purchase or sale of agricultural produce under the Rural Development Fund Act, 1987, which is executed by Punjab Rural Development Board. The market committees have been made the collecting agencies for the same.

Board of Directors

The Board of Directors of PSAMB consists of a Chairman nominated by the state government and 16 other members.

Official members (8)—representing the Department of Finance, Horticulture Agriculture Cooperation, Animal Husbandry, Colonisation, Food & Supplies, and Secretary of the Board.

Non-official members (8)—One shall be an agricultural producer member of a market committee, one shall be from among such persons licensed under section 10 as are members of a committee, one shall be from among such persons licensed under section 13 as are members of a committee, one shall be a member of a register organisation of farmers, three shall be progressive producers of Punjab, one from each division and one representing the cooperative societies.

Secretary of the Board shall be appointed by the state government from amongst the members of the Indian Administrative Services (IAS).

Term of the office of the non-official members of the Board shall be of three years.

Thrust Area

Provision/Strengthening of Marketing Infrastructure in Mandis

PSAMB has raised a loan of approximately ₹ 89 crore from Oriental Bank of Commerce for providing additional infrastructural facilities in various principal yards, sub-yards and purchase centres. This project will cover 53 market committees with development works at 178 different places in the state. The main components of this project are provision of *pucca* auction platforms, metalled roads, water supply, sewerage system, permanent electrification, drainage and construction of cover sheds on auction platforms in selective *mandis*. The Board is laying emphasis for provision of cover sheds in all important *mandis* to guard against inclement weather during the peak procurement time for paddy and wheat in order to minimise the losses to farmers as well as to government in the procurement operations. The Board is also contributing seed money in case of those market committees that are economically weak. By raising loan from banks for provision of additional infrastructure, the Board would be able to give facilities in the *mandis* within a period of two years, which in the normal course would have taken eight to ten years. This massive project would be completed by the end of June 2000.

Punjab Agricultural Export Corporation (PAGREXCO)

It was being felt for the last decade that some major initiatives are required for marketing of fruits and vegetables being grown in the state because of highly perishable nature of the produce. A major initiative was taken by the state government by establishing a separate corporation namely Punjab Agricultural Export Cooperation with PSAMB and Punjab Agro Industries Corporation, contributing 50 per cent equity each for the establishment of this Corporation. PAGREXCO is dedicated to promoting export of fruits and vegetables outside the country and also to the distant markets within the country, in order to help the farmers to realise better returns for their produce.

Punjab Horticulture Post Harvest Technology Centre

In order to minimise the post-harvest losses, the state government has established Post Harvest Technology Centre at Punjab Agricultural University, Ludhiana, with the financial assistance of PSAMB. The basic purpose of this centre is to develop techniques for increasing the shelf life of horticultural and vegetable produce and to impart training to the producers, traders and concerned government department employees for proper handling, grading, storage, packaging and transportation of produce. This will benefit the growers as well as traders to improve quality and minimise losses of fruit and vegetables in the state, ultimately benefiting the consumers.

Arranging Loans for Development Works of Market Committees

The board and market committees are committed to provide infrastructure in the field of agricultural marketing. To achieve this goal, special project has been finalised to arrange loan of ₹ 78.87 crore for 52 market committees from Oriental Bank of Commerce. The projected amount earmarked for this purpose is ₹ 100.64 crore.

Conclusions and Suggestions

Conclusions

The following conclusions can be drawn on the basis of the analysis:

- KSAMB is dependent on the contributions from the APMC for carrying out their activities. The contributions from the APMCs have been increasing year on year.
- The grants from the government is also a significant source of income for the Board.
- Raitha Sanjeevani scheme is also bringing in a significant amount of money to the Board.
- The income from the printing press, *Krishipete* magazine, and interest on APMC loans are the other major sources of revenue for the Board.
- Employee compensation and Raitha Sanjeevani schemes are the major expenditures for the Board.
- Maratavahini disseminates relevant information about different agricultural commodities to the farmers.
- Introduction of toll-free telephone number system for providing information about the prices of various commodities at different markets is a huge success with the farmers.
- KSAMB gets 1 per cent as market fee on all transactions of APMCs. PSAMB gets 2 per cent as fee on transactions of APMCs.

- PSAMB exercises superintendence and control over the APMCs. KSAMB's role *vis-à-vis* APMCs is advisory in nature.

Suggestions

The following suggestions are offered for consideration by GoK:

- KSAMB's success depends upon the success of the APMCs. It should initiate awareness programmes in the villages, so that more and more farmers sell their produce at APMCs.
- Role clarity and proper coordination is required between the Board and APMC. The director can play the role of a catalyst in achieving coordination so that effectiveness of the programmes can be improved.
- The welfare programmes of the Board are popular and are creating good will among the farmers. The Board can initiate more such programmes.
- More toll-free telephone numbers have to be introduced so as to cater to the needs of larger number of farmers.
- KSAMB should initiate more number of training programmes so as to cover a large number of farmers about grading and post-harvest technologies.
- KSAMB is playing an advisory role. It can be given a bigger role in implementation of schemes/initiatives.
- The contributions from APMCs to KSAMB should be increased. The fee for all transactions in APMCs can be increased from 1 per cent to 2 per cent, as is the case in Punjab.

KSAMB plays a passive and advisory role *vis-à-vis* APMCs. The role of KSAMB can be redefined so as to make them more assertive and lead to the better marketing of agricultural products in Karnataka.

The role and relevance of KSAMB is very high, as it is providing good inputs for marketing of agricultural produce. The welfare activities undertaken for the farmers and *hamalis* in the state should be continued and expanded in scope. Hence, the KSAMB should be allowed to continue albeit with some redefining of roles and restructuring to make it more effective.

Training activities, which is one of main functions of the Board has to be increased. Research and rural development activities should be given additional focus.

Maratavahini is providing up-to-date information about prices of agriculture commodities in different districts of the state. The Board should be made as a nodal agency to improve the IT facilities for the benefit of the farmers, and also to impart the required IT training for the farmers.